Frontier shelf

976

X

D1526373

The M. K. Brown Range Life Series, No. 15

C. C. Slaughter

C. C. Slaughter
Rancher, Banker, Baptist

By David J. Murrah

University of Texas Press, Austin

First Edition, 1981

Requests for permission to reproduce material from this work should be sent to Permissions, University of Texas Press, Box 7819, Austin, Texas 78712.

Library of Congress Cataloging in Publication Data

Murrah, David J.
  C. C. Slaughter, rancher, banker, Baptist.
  (M. K. Brown range life series)
  Includes index.
  1. Slaughter, C. C. 2. Ranch life—Texas. 3. Ranchers—Texas—Biography. 4. Bankers—Texas—Biography. 5. Baptists—Texas—Biography. 6. Texas—Biography. I. Title.
II. Series.
F391.S627M87 976.4'061-0924 [B] 81-1661
ISBN 0-292-71067-4   AACR2

In memory of my father, Roy Murrah

Contents

Preface

Trail driver, Texas Ranger, banker, philanthropist, and cattleman, Christopher Columbus Slaughter (1837–1919) was in his day one of America's most famous ranchers. Long before oil made many West Texans rich, Slaughter amassed a four-million-dollar fortune through successful manipulation of land, labor, and capital. He learned entrepreneurial skill on the Texas frontier; that same frontier, however, tested its student as Indian attacks, recurring drought, and unpredictable winters often presented Slaughter with difficult challenges. Born during the infant years of the Texas Republic, he participated in the development of the southwestern cattle industry from its pioneer stages to the modern era. A pioneer in West Texas ranching, Slaughter increased his holdings from 1877 to 1905 to include more than a million acres of land and forty thousand head of cattle. At one time "Slaughter country" stretched from a few miles north of Big Spring northwestward two hundred miles to the New Mexico border west of Lubbock. His family, including his father, brothers, and sons, rode the crest of popularity he established; and the Slaughter name virtually became a household word in the Southwest. In 1873, almost ten years before the highly profitable "beef bonanza" on the open range had made many Texas cattlemen rich, a Dallas newspaper called C. C. Slaughter "the Cattle King of Texas."

Although Slaughter is a legendary figure in the state, historians, hampered by the absence of any personal papers and business records, overlooked or avoided undertaking a significant study of his career. In 1966, however, Don W. Slaughter of Lubbock donated approximately one thousand letters of correspondence between his grandfather, George M. Slaughter, and his great-grandfather, C. C. Slaughter, to the Southwest Collection at Texas Tech University. These letters, saved from destruction by Don's uncle, the late Jo Dick Slaughter of Lubbock, were written from 1893 to 1910. Although covering only seventeen years of C. C. Slaughter's sixty-five-year career as a Texas cattleman, the correspondence led to the discovery of other significant materials.

During the course of this study, I became indebted to many people: Don Slaughter; his mother, Mrs. George M. Slaughter II, of Roswell, New Mexico; Mrs. Anella Bauer; Mr. and Mrs. Jimmy De-Loache of Dallas; other members of the Slaughter family who graciously contributed valuable information; Mr. and Mrs. W. D. O'Brien of Lubbock and Mr. and Mrs. Courtney Sanders of Morton, who generously provided financial assistance for the preparation of the final copy of the manuscript; and the members of the staff of the Southwest Collection, who courteously assisted beyond the bounds of their official duties.

I am also indebted to Texas Tech University Professors Jacquelin Collins, Harry A. Jebsen, Jr., Joseph E. King, Kline A. Nall, and the late David M. Vigness, for their helpful criticism. I am especially grateful to Professor Emeritus Ernest Wallace for his invaluable advice. Special thanks also go to my wife, Ann, and children, Donna, Elaine, and Jerel, for their help, understanding, and encouragement.

David J. Murrah

C. C. Slaughter

1

Frontier
Beginnings

As word of the election of Abraham Lincoln in November 1860 spread throughout the South, thousands of young men rallied to defend their native states. Even on the western frontier of Texas, far removed from cotton fields and slaves, war fever ran high. There young Christopher Columbus Slaughter enthusiastically joined his friends and neighbors in forming a local militia company being organized for North Texas frontier defense. The impending conflict provided an opportunity for adventure, glory, and perpetuation of a long family tradition of militia service. Slaughter remembered the stories his father had told of serving under Sam Houston during the Texas Revolution in 1836; he recalled his grandfather's accounts of being with Andrew Jackson at the battle of New Orleans in 1815; he knew of his great-grandfather's service in a North Carolina militia unit during the American Revolution. Since his ancestors had already served as frontier militiamen in three American wars, young Slaughter proudly responded to the call for volunteers.

Three preceding generations of Slaughters had experienced a century of American frontier life. The family line can be traced to the eighteenth-century Virginia frontier, but documenting its origin in America appears to be impossible. The Slaughters of Texas may have originated in America with a Richard Slaughter who settled in Nansemond County, Virginia, in the early seventeenth century. According to a family genealogist, Elmer Cunningham Slaughter, within a century

Richard Slaughter's descendants apparently had migrated through Bertie County into Lunenburg County, Virginia. Walter Slaughter, C. C. Slaughter's great-grandfather, was born about 1750, possibly in Lunenburg County. A planter, Walter settled in Anson County in southwestern North Carolina during the late 1700s. At the outbreak of the American Revolution in 1775, Walter enlisted in Captain Thomas Wade's light horse cavalry, a minuteman battalion, and served until he was captured by the British. After his release, about 1780, he left military service and returned home to marry Margaret Webb. Walter and Margaret had six children, including two adventurous sons, John and William.[1]

As cotton planters, Walter and his sons participated in the rush for new and fertile lands in the South. In the 1780s the Slaughters moved to Washington County, Georgia. After William married Nancy Moore in Amite County, Mississippi, the entire family moved in 1810 to Lawrence County, Mississippi, west of the Pearl River and north of the American-Spanish border. There Walter and his sons engaged in both farming and stock raising. William and his brother John supported their neighbor frontiersmen in the eviction of the Spaniards from Baton Rouge and participated in Andrew Jackson's defense of New Orleans against the British in 1815.

William then followed his younger brother Robert to Hinds County, Mississippi, near present-day Jackson, and in 1821 to Copiah County. By 1825 William and Nancy had several children, including three sons, George Webb, born in 1811, Samuel Moore, in 1818, and William Ransom, in 1825. Soon after the birth of the latter, William, having heard the numerous stories of abundant and unbelievably cheap virgin land in Texas, with Nancy and the children set out by wagon for the land of greater opportunity. For some reason, however, he settled in Sabine Parish, Louisiana, a few miles east of the Texas border. Perhaps, since he was a strong Protestant, he had developed some reservations about having to become a Catholic in a Mexican state, or perhaps he preferred the protection that nearby Fort Jessup afforded.[2]

Young George Slaughter, however, could not resist the bustling activity beyond the Sabine and at eighteen began freighting goods across the river to San Augustine and Nacogdoches. George's stories about Texas influenced his father to move across the river in 1830, probably before the passage of the Law of April 6, 1830, that forbade the further immigration of Americans into Texas. Settling on one square league (4,428 acres) in Sabine County (to which he received title on August 16, 1835), William not only continued to grow cotton but also found the gentle hills of East Texas well suited for stock raising.

Political trouble soon disturbed the peaceful life in Texas. When Mexican Colonel José de las Piedras intimidated Texas colonists by threatening to ally his garrison at Nacogdoches with nearby Cherokee Indians, the settlers, including young George Slaughter, took up arms to drive the Mexican soldiers from East Texas. On July 31, 1832, fighting erupted in the narrow streets of Nacogdoches, and after two days of skirmishing, the Texans forced the Mexican troops to surrender.

For George Slaughter, the battle served as an initiation into frontier violence and probably prompted him to quit the drudgery of cotton fields for a more exciting career. As new settlers poured into eastern Texas following the cessation of the 1832 hostilities, he freighted their goods between Louisiana and Nacogdoches, and by the fall of 1833, his business was sufficiently reputable that newcomer Sam Houston hired him to transport his personal legal library from Louisiana to Nacogdoches.[3]

After initial shots of the Texas Revolution were fired at Gonzales on October 2, 1835, George joined Stephen F. Austin's volunteer army assembling in the San Antonio vicinity. On November 26 he participated in the so-called Grass Fight, an engagement in which the Texans captured a Mexican pack train loaded with hay. He became a courier for Sam Houston in January 1836 and presumably delivered a message to William B. Travis at the Alamo. During the six-week period following its fall, Slaughter reportedly served as a procurer for Houston's army.

After Houston's victory at San Jacinto on April 21, Slaughter returned home to see about his family. Soon after his arrival, he became engaged to eighteen-year-old Sarah Mason; the couple delayed their wedding, apparently because of the absence of any civil law. Within a short time, Slaughter was again serving as a procurer for the growing army of Texas. He continued in this service until October. By that time Texas had adopted a constitution, elected a president, and established some semblance of law. As soon as his service with the army ended, Slaughter hastened home and on October 12, 1836, married Sarah Mason, who was five months pregnant. When the child was born the following February 11, the young parents named him Christopher Columbus, apparently in commemoration of their wedding date.[4]

After his marriage Slaughter resumed his freighting business for settlers and the new government. The influx of immigrants, however, led to conflict with the Cherokees that eventually erupted into war. For Slaughter the conflict marked his third call to military action in seven years. In July 1839 he joined with other volunteers under the command of Thomas Rusk to invade Indian lands in present-day Cherokee County.

After the Cherokee War, George Slaughter returned to Sabine County to pursue farming interests jointly with his father. While there he and Sarah had four additional children. In 1844 he entered the Baptist ministry, a career that would make him famous on the Texas frontier.[5]

But it was cattle rather than converts that perpetuated the Slaughter name in Texas. By the 1840s a growing Texas population and a fairly close New Orleans provided a new market for cattle. George Slaughter, quickly seeing an economic opportunity, began to use part of his land for stock raising. He later acquired three thousand acres, much of which he dedicated to that purpose. His herd grew slowly; by 1850 it probably numbered less than a hundred head.

Although Slaughter's cattle at first provided the family with only a secondary income, the small herd grazing the hills of Sabine County seemed of immense importance to young Christopher Columbus. While learning to castrate and brand cattle, he also learned to appreciate life on the open range.

In 1849 George, his brother William, and twelve-year-old C. C. (then known as "Lum" to family and friends) drove ninety-two head of cattle to a new ranch located along the banks of the Trinity River in Freestone County, 175 miles west of the Sabine settlements. The drive provided the Slaughters with valuable experience. Although trailing was nothing new, most herds were moved from farm to market along north-south river routes. The Slaughters, on the other hand, drove their cattle across the Angelina, Neches, and Trinity rivers, thereby providing opportunity for C. C. to begin developing an expertise in trail driving that eventually became a basic tool in the creation of a family fortune.

Leaving William with the cattle, George and C. C. returned to their farming interests. However, the death of George's father in April 1850 helped sever the family's tie to Sabine County. Furthermore, by 1852 raising cattle appeared more financially attractive than growing cotton on the worn-out soils of East Texas. At least, it was worth a try. Therefore, George Webb Slaughter, who by then had four sons, C. C., George, Peter, and John, headed west in 1852 with his family and possessions to the valley of the Trinity in southern Freestone County.[6]

The Trinity River valley provided ample grass for Slaughter cattle. Each year the family drove small herds to Shreveport for shipment to New Orleans. Because their ranch was near the fork of the Trinity on the Shreveport Trail, young C. C. was often employed by drovers from the west to help them get their herds across the frequently high river.

Freestone County offered other opportunities for C. C. In 1854, after finishing his education at Larissa College, a Presbyterian boarding school in Cherokee County, he set out on a three-month trading venture. Borrowing his father's wagon, he drove east to the pine forests near Palestine, purchased a load of lumber, hauled it to sparsely settled Dallas County, and sold it to incoming settlers for a profit. Slaughter then drove north to Collin County near McKinney and bought a load of wheat. By using his own team at a gristmill, he ground the wheat into flour, bagged and loaded it, and pointed his team southward. After pausing briefly at home, young Slaughter drove south another hundred miles to Magnolia, where he sold his last bag of flour. During a three-month period, he had traveled by wagon four hundred miles and netted a handsome $520 profit. With the money, he purchased his uncle's interest in his father's herd. Thus began a partnership that continued for more than twenty years.[7]

Meanwhile, Freestone County had filled rapidly with settlers, who by 1855 had converted over 250,000 acres to cotton production. Grass had become scarce. Furthermore, for several years the Slaughters had noticed that cattle from the Brazos River valley were fleshier and larger than their own and had heard that farther west ample grass and water were available. The potential lured young Slaughter westward as it had his father more than twenty-five years before. By the spring of 1855, C. C. had convinced his father that they should explore the Brazos and other westward streams for a new ranch.

For two months during the summer of 1855, the Slaughters roamed over hundreds of miles of West Texas grasslands, even penetrating the hunting grounds of Comanche and Kiowa Indians. Because of the newly established line of frontier defense posts, the Plains Indians were relatively peaceful that summer.

The Slaughters went west to the Brazos, possibly striking it near Fort Graham in Hill County, ten miles west of present-day Hillsboro. There they turned northwestward along its banks as far as Fort Belknap. Then, probably along the established military roads, they moved west to the Colorado River valley and explored where no cattlemen had been.[8]

The Slaughters' choice of a new range was not difficult. Although the virgin Colorado valley appeared to be a cattlemen's haven, it was also the home of both buffalo and Indians. The upper Brazos country in Palo Pinto and Young counties, however, offered both lush grass and military protection. Lying in the western Cross Timbers, the Brazos valley provided a broken, well-watered terrain; tough mountain cedar, Spanish oak, cottonwood, ash, and pecan trees offered ample material for housing and fencing; nearby Fort Belknap promised military security. In addition, two nearby Indian reservations, the Brazos Reservation for the Wichita and other East Texas sedentary tribes and the Comanche Reservation on the Clear Fork of the Brazos, offered a ready market for cattle. Also, other settlers along the Brazos—the Cowdens, Daltons, Goodnights, and Lovings—shared the Slaughters' enthusiasm for cattle raising.

George Webb Slaughter bought, for what became his final home, 2,900 acres along a sharp bend in the Brazos, four miles north of the tiny settlement of Golconda (now Palo Pinto) in Palo Pinto County. In 1856 C. C. drove the Slaughter cattle north to the new ranch and supervised the building of a new home. The next year the entire family, which by this time included seven children, completed the move from Freestone County and settled in the new log cabin.[9]

The Slaughters' new home lay in the heart of the North Texas frontier. Although a county government had been created in 1854, three years before the arrival of the Slaughter family, the region was still thinly populated. Fort Belknap was thirty miles west of the Slaughter home, and according to Charles Goodnight, "nothing [lay] west from there to the Rocky Mountains."

Because of the isolation, the Slaughters and other frontier cattlemen were able to take advantage of the market for beef created by the nearby fort and Indian reserves. Fort Belknap, on the busy Butterfield

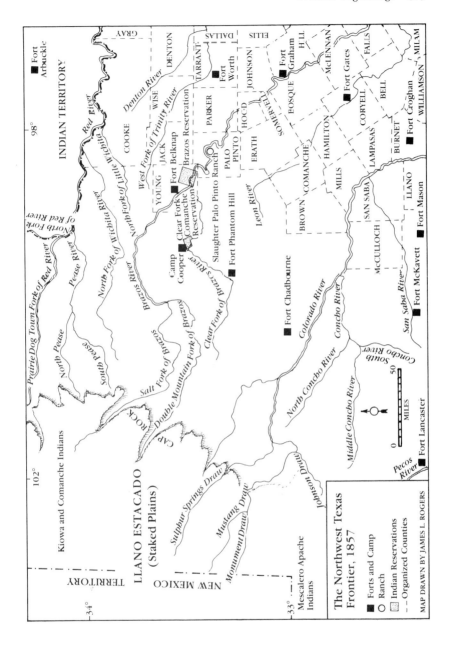

The Northwest Texas Frontier, 1857

■ Forts and Camp
○ Ranch
▨ Indian Reservations
-- Organized Counties

MAP DRAWN BY JAMES L. ROGERS

Overland Mail Route, was occupied by one to four companies of soldiers, all of whom savored the taste of fresh beef. The Brazos and Clear Fork reservations, which had approximately fourteen hundred Indians, also required a good beef supply. Through contractors, in 1857 the federal government purchased about thirty-four head weekly at a cost of $3.98 per hundred pounds. The sales added more than $25,000 annually to the frontier cattlemen's economy.[10]

In spite of their importance to cattlemen, the reservations soon became the focal point for alarm. In 1857 the United States Second Cavalry withdrew to Utah. Almost immediately Nokoni Comanches began raiding frontier settlements from Palo Pinto southward. Reprisal raids by federal and state troops into the heart of the Indian country along the Canadian River near the Texas-Oklahoma line incited additional Comanche forays. As a result many settlers either blamed reservation Indians for the attacks or accused them of sheltering raiding parties. By the end of 1858, the frontier was poised for full-scale war.

The Slaughters and other Palo Pinto cattlemen defended their friendly Indian neighbors on the Brazos Reservation and resisted any attempts to punish them. In December 1858, however, a party of about twenty frontiersmen from counties south of Palo Pinto determined to settle the problem. The mob, led by Peter Garland of Erath County, vowed to kill all Indians found off the reserve.

Meanwhile, a band of twenty-seven Caddo and other reservation Indians, under the leadership of Choctaw Tom, an old and peaceful chief, had left the Brazos Reservation to hunt game along the river. Encouraged by friendly Palo Pinto residents to stay in the area to hunt bear, the Indians camped on December 27 only one mile from the Slaughter Ranch. There the party of Erath County settlers surprised and killed seven of the sleeping Indians, including Choctaw Tom's wife and daughter.[11]

Awakened by gunfire, C. C. Slaughter hurried to the scene. When he determined what had happened, he rushed home, saddled a horse, and headed for the reservation. He always remembered the incident.

> I knew instinctively that what few Indians had escaped would immediately return to the agency . . . and [then] return before daylight to bury their dead and afterwards wreak a most horrible revenge on the innocent people of that settlement for an act committed by a lot of hotheaded thoughtless men from an entirely different section of the country. I determined to prevent this second outrage if possible.

Young Slaughter was in the most dangerous situation he had ever faced. After riding two-thirds of the way, he encountered a large band of hostile Indians. "They were covered with war paint and in the ugliest frame of mind," Slaughter remembered. Personally acquainted with a number of the leaders, he explained the situation and tried to assure the Indians that the residents of Palo Pinto were innocent. "By constantly talking in this vein and assisting them in the burial of their dead, I eventually succeeded in quieting them for the time being," he said. "I shall always firmly believe, however, that had I not interceded on this occasion there would have been one of the most horrible massacres ever perpetrated by savage vengeance." Slaughter's midnight intervention was not in vain. Within two days Palo Pinto settlers had formed a defense, but no attack ever came. Unfortunately, the murderers went unpunished.

The settler-Indian conflict doomed the Texas reservations. Agitated by former Indian agent John R. Baylor, many of the frontier's citizens demanded that the Indians be removed from Texas. In May 1859 Baylor assembled an "Army of Defense" and, without authority, moved against the Brazos Reservation. After a brief skirmish, the invaders withdrew, but the incident provoked the federal government into removing the Indians from Texas. In spite of protests by several frontier ranchers, 1,535 occupants of the two Texas reservations were escorted northward across the Red River in August 1859.[12]

The removal did little to halt Indian raids along the Texas frontier. Especially hard hit were Jack, Young, Palo Pinto, and Parker counties, where Indians stole "all the horses they could get." The resulting discontent was a major factor in incumbent Governor Hardin Runnels' defeat by Sam Houston in the 1859 election. Citizens of Palo Pinto and the frontier immediately asked Houston for relief from the depredations.

Houston tried to take steps to improve the situation. He called upon the federal government for additional troops and supplies; he dispatched seven companies of Texas Rangers to northwest Texas; and in March 1860 he authorized the organization of minutemen companies of fifteen men each in twenty-three frontier counties. Although Houston's maneuvers quickly brought a measure of peace, the November 1860 election of Abraham Lincoln, the subsequent secession of Texas from the Union and the withdrawal of federal troops from North Texas, unbeknown to the Slaughters and other cattlemen, would soon create an even worse situation on the frontier.

Before the Civil War, the Slaughters had done well during their four years on the frontier. By 1860 more than a thousand head of cattle carried the Slaughter brand. Owning the second largest herd in the county as well as four thousand acres of land along the Brazos, George Webb and C. C. claimed a modest estate valued at twenty thousand dollars. Their cattle holdings had increased 300 percent during the 1850s.[13]

Until the outbreak of hostilities between settlers and Indians, frontier life for the Slaughters followed a set pattern: father George Webb Slaughter preached the gospel while his boys cared for the cattle. The elder Slaughter, who had only three weeks of formal education, had been shepherding small Baptist congregations for more than ten years before his move to Palo Pinto County. He soon became well known on the northwestern Texas frontier for his fiery and forceful preaching.

Near his home in 1858, he built the Slaughter Valley Baptist Church, the first in the county, and later founded other congregations in Palo Pinto, Mineral Wells, and adjoining communities. Even with hostile Indians in the country, he weekly followed a sixty-mile circuit with a Bible and a hymnbook in his saddle, often preaching with revolver and carbine within reach. In spite of his pastoral manner, Slaughter founded fifty churches and baptized three thousand persons during his fifty-year ministry. Before he retired in 1886, he was far better known as an itinerant preacher than as a cattleman.

Cattle, however, were just as important to Slaughter as converts. On one occasion a small Baptist congregation had gathered at its church to hear the well-known preacher, who had failed to appear at the appointed hour. Late in the evening, Slaughter arrived and quickly explained to the faithful few who had waited that he had encountered several unbranded calves along the way that needed his brand.

Even though his ministerial services were appreciated by his neighbors, at least on one occasion they could not resist having fun with the aging cattleman-preacher. "One Sunday morning when the Reverend was preaching a warm and lengthy sermon under a brush arbor some cowboys ran a small bunch of mavericks down on the meeting place. Frightened, the animals dashed through the aisle and among the benches. The incident did not particularly excite Reverend Slaughter, but he did not forget the boys in his closing prayer. He called on the Lord 'to hold them over the fires of hell, take them by the neck, let them dangle over the fiery furnace, but, oh Lord, don't let them drop.'"[14]

While their father was preaching, C. C. and his younger brothers, George, Pete, and John, tended the cattle herds. The operation also required the occasional hiring of at least two extra men. Because there were no fences, the family conducted periodic "cow hunts" in order to gather cattle out of the brushy Brazos River breaks. Then they drove selected stock to the Slaughter holding pens they had constructed five miles east of the Brazos Reservation. From there the Slaughters delivered cattle to the contractor supplying the Indian reserve.

The lucrative Slaughter cattle trade was completely disrupted by the outbreak of hostilities between frontier settlers and Indians. The 1859 removal of the reservation Indians, coupled with the periodic attacks upon their horse and cattle herds, not only cut off their principal market but also forced the Slaughters to keep their cattle penned close to the home ranch.

A tragic death also marred the family operation. In June 1860 C. C.'s younger brother George was killed when he became entangled in a rope tied to a runaway mule. Although he was only seventeen, the boy was an invaluable part of the Slaughter cattle business; his death heralded the beginning of a dismal decade.[15]

Coinciding with George's death were renewed Indian raids, especially in Palo Pinto County. C. C. Slaughter soon found himself chasing more Indians than cattle. Frustrated by lack of protection from federal and state forces, he joined with ninety-four other young settlers on December 5, 1860, to form a volunteer Ranger company. Once assembled in eastern Young County, the citizen soldiers elected as captain J. J. ("Jack") Cureton, a veteran of the Brazos reserve skirmish of 1859. On December 12 the settlers joined with a state Ranger company commanded by young Lawrence Sullivan Ross. Then reinforced by twenty-three U.S. Army dragoons from Camp Cooper, the Texans, under Ross' command, set out toward Indian country.

The expedition gave C. C. Slaughter opportunity to preview virgin cattle country, an experience that would be of immense value in later years. The column's route traversed the rolling breaks of the Little Wichita and Big Wichita rivers near present-day Vernon. Finally, fourteen miles west of Vernon, Ross' Ranger company surprised a Comanche camp. Without waiting for the larger body of volunteers to join his troops, Ross ordered an immediate attack and killed twelve in the band, including Chief No-bah (Nocona?) in hand-to-hand combat.[16]

Slaughter and the other volunteers missed the battle by minutes. Charles Goodnight, who was serving as a scout, arrived in time to see the final minutes of action. He then turned to watch Slaughter and the others straggle to the site. "With their tin cups, pans and guns glistening in the bright sun," Goodnight remembered, "they made a thrilling sight that was very impressive. I regret to say that there were some good horses behind, but probably the riders' appetites were not craving for lead."

When Slaughter and the others arrived, they found the place strewn with packets of buffalo robes, blankets, tents, food supplies, and other materials the Indians had preserved for winter survival. There they also saw prisoners taken during the skirmish—a woman, a boy, and a little girl. The capture of the woman made Ross and the expedition famous. While being questioned, the woman exclaimed in broken English, "Me Cynthia Ann." In 1836 Cynthia Ann Parker, then nine years of age, had been captured by Comanches during a raid on Parker's Fort on the Navasota River near present-day Groesbeck. Afterward she was hunted by family and friends, and by the time of her rescue, her name had become legendary. The story of the battle and her release was later told by Ross and published throughout the state.[17]

While chasing Indians proved to be exciting, C. C. Slaughter quickly learned that such adventures were incompatible with cattle raising. By the time he returned home on January 1, he found that in his absence Indians had stolen forty of the ranch's best horses. Fortunately, the family had survived the raid by barricading themselves in their homes. Even more appalling to Slaughter was the news that Republican Abraham Lincoln had been elected president of the United States. "The fact has caused great excitement among the people," Slaughter's neighbor, J. II. Baker, recorded, "and they are in for secession."

The Palo Pinto settlers were eager for action. Because of the renewed Indian threat, or perhaps responding to a growing secession fever, Palo Pinto County's chief justice, R. W. Pollard, on January 14, 1861, issued a call for the formation of a fifteen-man Ranger company to patrol the borders of the county. On January 19 young men of the county gathered at Palo Pinto for enlistment. Following initial enrollment, the volunteers elected officers. C. C. Slaughter was chosen lieutenant. His election, however, was not unanimous. "I opposed his election as I do not consider him suitable for that office," recorded

J. H. Baker. "I have but little confidence of the company's doing any good, but hope for the best." For his service Slaughter was to receive ninety-five dollars a month.[18]

Although Slaughter's company was ordered to scout and protect only its home county, secession fever in Texas soon altered the nature of its service. On February 1, 1861, an Austin convention overwhelmingly approved an ordinance of secession. When the news reached the frontier, the settlers took prompt action. At Camp Cooper, located on the Clear Fork of the Brazos thirty-two miles west of Fort Belknap and occupied by two hundred fifty U.S. Army regulars, approximately two hundred armed Texans assembled, intending to take the post, if necessary, by force. Included in the Texas camp were six companies of Rangers, several armed bands of volunteers, and, although it was many miles from home, the Palo Pinto Ranger Company commanded by C. C. Slaughter.

Wisely, the commander of the U.S. troops, Captain S. D. Carpenter, decided not to challenge the heavily armed Texans. On February 21 his troops began a withdrawal to San Antonio, escorted by Slaughter's Palo Pinto company. However, near Camp Colorado, six miles northeast of Coleman, the Palo Pinto Rangers turned aside to follow a fresh Indian trail. Finding no Indians, they returned to Camp Cooper. When their term of service expired in April, they returned home to learn that state troops had successfully removed all federal troops from the state, that Texas had joined the Confederacy, and that war had begun.[19]

On February 7, 1861, the Texas legislature created a new law for frontier defense, providing for companies of forty men to be raised in each county. Ten men were to be kept in the field as "spies"; service was not to exceed ten days at any one time. This arrangement was both necessary and satisfactory to the frontiersmen, for it allowed them to remain at home, many miles from the war in the East, and to protect their families and livestock.

The outbreak of the war affected young C. C. Slaughter only slightly. Eager to rebuild his cattle and horse herds which had been depleted during his absence, he chose not to join one of the many companies being raised to fight Yankees. Furthermore, having completed almost four months of frontier Ranger service under Ross and with his own command, the young cattleman felt no obligation to reenroll in a minuteman company.

During the first months of the war, the frontier remained relatively quiet, thanks to the diplomacy of the newly established Confederate States of America. On August 12, 1861, Commissioner Albert Pike successfully negotiated treaties with the Comanches, Kiowas, and Wichitas which brought a temporary peace to the Texas frontier. C. C. Slaughter quickly took advantage of the period of peace. With the aid of his father, he began to enlarge his cattle holdings. Because the war offered a potential market for Texas beef, the Slaughters bought cattle at every opportunity. They marketed stock through neighboring drovers, including Oliver Loving, who were commissioned to supply the Confederacy with beef. Loving, who had herded cattle to Illinois and Colorado before the war, drove beeves throughout the war to various points on the Mississippi River.[20]

The frontier peace also afforded young Slaughter another opportunity. Soon after his return home from Ranger service, the twenty-four-year-old cattleman began courting Cynthia Jowell, the seventeen-year-old daughter of George Slaughter's neighboring rancher, James A. Jowell. The couple set Thursday, December 5, 1861, for the wedding. Held at the Jowell home in the evening, the ceremony was elaborate for a frontier wedding in the midst of war. J. H. Baker, who was a candlebearer and consequently enjoyed a front row advantage, summarized the proceedings in his diary.

> It was announced that all was ready and we appeared on the floor. Miss Nan and I led the way, the other attendants next, followed by the bride and groom. There were several awkward moves before we were placed right. However, all was finally satisfactory and the ceremony was performed by S. A. Oxford, Esq. We were then ushered into the dining room where we partook of a fine supper.

Although Baker enjoyed the initial celebration, he saw no usefulness in the party that followed at the Jowell home.

> The remainder of the night was spent until 11 pm in conversation and various foolish games. As soon as I was relieved of my responsibilities, I came home, feeling I had spent the time quite unprofitably. . . . The rabble attempted to get up a regular chaviriri [sic], but failed. They fired several guns, blew a bugle, and yelled around the house a few times, but did not get their bells and other noises started, and consequently considered it a failure. It is a shameful practice and ought to be stopped.

On the following day the groom's family hosted the customary "infair" dinner. From the Jowell home, a huge throng moved in an elegant procession to the village school, where two hundred guests consumed, according to Baker, "a very good dinner—the best I have seen in Texas."[21]

The ceremonies completed, Slaughter settled his bride in a simple log cabin near his father's ranch. There their first child, George Morgan, was born on November 2, 1862. Soon, however, his family's comfortable life on the frontier ended. One day while C. C. was driving cattle, a small party of Comanches who no longer adhered to their treaty trapped Slaughter's young wife in her house. Pretending to want food, the Indians crowded around the door until Cynthia opened it slightly to hand them some of her cooking. One Indian attempted to push into the room but was stopped by a shotgun blast that struck him in the chest. Fearing that the sound of the shot would bring quick aid to the lone housewife, the other Indians fled. When he returned home a few hours later, C. C. found a distraught wife and on his doorstep a dead Comanche. For the duration of the war, he housed his wife and son near the stockade at Palo Pinto.

Indian attacks remained imminent as the withdrawal of federal troops left the frontier unprotected. In an attempt to provide security, the Texas legislature in December 1861 created the Frontier Regiment consisting of nine companies manned by residents of the frontier counties. Although many settlers quickly volunteered for service, C. C. Slaughter, with a new bride at home, did not enroll in the initial enlistment but possibly participated in scouting activity on a voluntary basis.[22]

Although the presence of the Frontier Regiment brought a brief respite from Indian raids, the peace collapsed near the end of 1862. On October 23 Comanche Indians, agitated by federal agents, destroyed the Confederate Wichita Indian Agency and, by the following spring, were poised once again to raid Texas settlements. The Indians soon learned to slip through the Frontier Regiment's line of defense. On February 28, 1863, two men were killed near the village of Palo Pinto by a party of Indians who were returning from a raid in adjoining Parker County. For the Slaughters and their neighbors, who were attempting to hold their cattle herds together, maintenance of life and property became even more difficult. Forced to combine their firepower and foodstocks, the Slaughters "forted up" with neighbors in a small stockade in Palo Pinto when Indian raids were imminent.

As the months passed, Indian depredations increased in the region in spite of the continued presence of the Frontier Regiment. In an attempt to deal with the deteriorating situation, the Texas legislature in December 1863 again changed the system of frontier defense. The new law provided for the enrollment of all persons liable for military duty residing in the frontier counties, including Palo Pinto, into companies of twenty-five to sixty-five men. On February 2, 1864, C. C. Slaughter enlisted in the District One regiment as a private in Company A of Young County's First Frontier Regiment under the command of Captain William Peveler. From February to October, he alternated duty with his neighbors, serving ten days out of every forty. Concerned primarily with scouting for Indians in the Fort Belknap area, the citizen-soldiers soon were confronted with a new enemy, deserters and Kansas Jayhawkers. These men, many of whom had fled from the South's deteriorating armies, sought refuge on the isolated frontier. Their presence made work for the military difficult. Occasionally, arrests were made, but growing sympathy for deserters in the waning months of the war, especially in North Texas, prevented rigorous enforcement of law. On the other hand, the Jayhawkers and deserters were helpful to the Rangers, for they made the northern frontier of Texas unsafe for Indians. These two deterrents combined with an even greater factor—the outbreak of a Plains Indian war from Texas to Canada against the United States—enabled the North Texas frontier to escape with very few Indian raids during the final year of the war.[23]

As a member of the Frontier Regiment, C. C. Slaughter was better able to help his father and brothers protect their homes and cattle. And because many of their neighbors sold or abandoned their herds during that time, the Slaughters were able to increase their holdings. One unfortunate frontier incident renewed an old market for the Slaughters. In mid-July 1863 a remnant of the Tonkawas, who had escaped a tragic massacre of their kinsmen by Plains Indians in Indian Territory the previous year, returned to the old Brazos Reservation. Because of their previous success in dealing with Indians, the Slaughters obtained a contract to supply cattle periodically to the Tonkawas at their village. The wartime prosperity created by cattle sales naturally ended with the fall of the Confederacy. "We found the Confederate money received for the cattle furnished to the government for the Indians during the Civil

War had no value," C. C.'s younger brother Bill recalled. "It was turned over to the children attending the school to use as thumb paper for old Blue Back spellers of those days."[24]

When the war ended in the spring of 1865, the Slaughters were short on good money but long on cattle. However, it appeared for a time that their cattle were about as worthless as Confederate money. The war had totally disrupted the cattle market; Comanches and Kiowas renewed their raids against unprotected ranches and settlements, causing frontier residents to retreat eastward; and deserters and outlaws roamed through the country almost at will. Furthermore, military or carpetbagger rule seemed certain.

Obviously alarmed with the situation, C. C. Slaughter and several friends discussed alternatives. After several weeks of deliberation, the young Palo Pinto residents decided to locate a new cattle range, far from the thieving Indians and hated Yankees, possibly in Mexico. By the summer of 1865, the group, including Slaughter, his brother-in-law, John Richard ("Dick") Jowell, Kit Carter, George Lemley, Alfred Lane, and Lane's brother-in-law, Charles Goodnight, had made arrangements to scout for a suitable location.

From Palo Pinto the young cattlemen rode southwest. For the first few days, they pushed rapidly through the familiar rolling prairies to the Colorado River near present-day Brownwood. After exploring the Colorado River valley briefly, they turned south and crossed the San Saba River at the site of the old Spanish San Sabá Mission, near present-day Menard, that had been destroyed in 1758 by Comanches and their Wichita allies.

Although the San Saba valley appeared promising, the young Texans felt that they were not yet safely beyond Yankee rule. Therefore, they turned west, followed the San Saba to its headwaters, and then plunged into the semiarid broken country of Southwest Texas. Probably near present-day Sonora, they crossed the El Paso–San Antonio road, found water in Granger Draw, and followed its meandering course southward through the rolling brush-covered hills of Val Verde County to the Devil's River, only a few miles from the Rio Grande and Mexico.

There an accident ended the adventure. The group was riding single file through the cedar breaks when Lemley's gun became entangled in a low-hanging tree branch, causing the rifle to discharge. C. C. Slaughter, riding ahead of his friend, was in the line of fire. Striking him in the right shoulder, the ball lodged against his breastbone. Although they did not expect him to survive, his companions doctored the victim by pulling a silk handkerchief through the wound to stop the bleeding and then made camp on the banks of the inhospitable Devil's River, seemingly appropriately named, to await the outcome of the tragedy.

For almost four weeks, Slaughter lay in camp while his friends hunted food for the return trip. Finally, his wound healed enough, the group moved Slaughter on a litter to the nearest settlement, perhaps Camp Hudson, where he received medical attention. After an absence of several months, the adventurers arrived back in Palo Pinto in February 1866, more willing to face both Indians and carpetbaggers.

Slaughter remained an invalid for almost a year. Confined to his home, he watched helplessly while his cattle herds dwindled through theft by both whites and Indians. Disgusted, he offered to sell his entire holdings, including his home, cattle, land, and horses, for ten thousand dollars, but no one could afford to buy his interests, even though priced most reasonably.[25] At the time he did not realize that his family's endurance of frontier hardships would soon pay off. The war had created a new and expanded market for beef, and pecuniary rewards awaited those cattlemen who were fortunate enough to survive. He did not envision—even dare dream—that fifteen years later he would refuse a million dollars for his cattle empire.[26]

2

Cattleman and Banker

At the close of the Civil War, the Northwest Texas ranching frontier was in a deplorable condition. For almost two years thereafter, the Slaughters and their neighbors attempted to recover and maintain their herds without the benefit of military protection. Furthermore, the collapse of the southern economy destroyed both wartime fortunes and cattle markets. "Cattle were almost worthless," W. C. Cochran, one of the Slaughters' neighbors, remembered. "During the auful [*sic*] severe winters we had . . . , the cattle drifted from the Red River to the Rio Grande." Unbranded stock mingled with domestic herds throughout the frontier counties.

The situation invited what frontiersmen described as "the mavericking days." "It [branding unmarked livestock whose ownership was uncertain] was not considered stealing at that time," recalled one Palo Pinto pioneer. "Every man that could get together a little bunch of horses . . . hired a few men and went to work rounding up and branding every thing they could get and kept all they got." [1] Apparently, the Slaughters joined the scramble for unbranded animals. By the spring of 1866, C. C. had recovered from his wound sufficiently to join his father and brothers in rebuilding the family herd.

Indian raids, however, continued to reduce Slaughter stock. Comanches and Kiowas, attacking in small bands, struck at isolated ranches, driving away cattle and horses at will. Thirteen braves surprised George Slaughter east of present-day Graham in 1866 as he drove a small herd through the breaks of Dry Creek. By firing both his carbine and hand gun, the parson managed to escape. Such raids accounted for the loss of perhaps as many as 300,000 head of cattle from Texas during the eight years following the war. Jack County, bordering the Slaughters on the north, had 5,000 head of cattle in 1860 but only 78 a decade later. The Indians also prized horses and mules; in eight years they stole at least 6,255 head from thirty-nine frontier counties, including 259 from Jack, Young, and Palo Pinto.

Indian attacks also prolonged the settler exodus from the frontier that had begun at the outbreak of the war. At least seventy-eight whites were killed in 1866 in fourteen North Texas counties. The onslaught drove the frontier eastward. Jack County's population declined from 1,000 in 1860 to 694 in 1870, and Young County lost even more, from 592 to 155.

In 1867 frontier people finally got some relief. Federal troops were sent to North Texas to garrison posts at Belknap and newly established Fort Richardson at Jacksboro. This new protection gave the Slaughters an opportunity to seek new markets for their cattle. Prewar outlets for Texas stock were no longer available. Missouri lawlessness, coupled with that state's farmer opposition to the dreaded "Texas fever," had disrupted cattle drives. Known in Texas as "Spanish fever," this livestock disease was carried by ticks, but its means of communication was not generally known. The Texas longhorns seemed immune to the fever, but northern herds were severely affected, particularly after grazing pastures a Texas herd had previously occupied. "Naturally, stockmen in the areas contaminated by the Longhorns began to clamor against allowing Texas cattle to pass through their counties." [2]

Although Charles Goodnight and Oliver Loving had teamed to drive herds to New Mexico and Colorado in 1866, western markets were still hazardous. C. C. Slaughter, however, was desperate. Impressed with the Goodnight-Loving success, he suggested to his father that they combine to drive to Shreveport, where cattle could be shipped by steamer to New Orleans. Reluctantly, perhaps, the elder Slaughter agreed.

Although previous drives to Shreveport had been successfully made by Palo Pinto cattlemen, the Slaughters always had relied on Oliver Loving to drive their cattle. Loving, however, had been killed by Indians while driving a herd of cattle up the Pecos River to Fort Sumner, New Mexico. Thus, the Slaughters initiated plans for their own drive.

Agreeing to a two thirds and one third partnership under the name of Slaughter and Son, George and C. C. rounded up nine hundred head for the drive.

In addition to C. C. and his father, four hands were hired for the long trip, including C. C.'s fifteen-year-old brother Bill. In late spring the drive began. The Slaughters followed a well-worn trail which passed near Fort Worth and Dallas. At Dallas the drive was delayed by the flooded, mile-wide Trinity River.

Fortunately, the delay caused the Slaughters to change their destination, a decision that, perhaps, changed also their lives. While waiting for the Trinity to recede, the Slaughters encountered Colonel T. H. Johnson, who, with six hundred cattle, was likewise stranded. Johnson, who had a contract with a Jefferson packing plant, was anxious to reach his destination before his time limit expired. The Slaughters, experts in river crossings, were in an excellent position to bargain with Johnson. After some deliberation the Slaughter cattle were included in Johnson's drive, and Johnson's name was added to the Slaughter and Son partnership.

The swollen river then gave C. C. Slaughter an opportunity to apply the boyhood training gained more than ten years before while helping drovers cross the Trinity in Freestone County. His expertise paid off. With little loss he got both herds across.

C. C. and Johnson then left the herd and traveled ahead to Jefferson to complete the contract. Slowly, the elder Slaughter traced their path through muddy East Texas fields and pastures. Bill Slaughter never forgot the experience: "As soon as we struck the piney woods, we would place the herds in the fields overnight in order to get crop grass for them and the rainy season being on, we were continually having to pull them out of the quicksand in the mornings. When we arrived at the packery, we held the cattle there about two weeks until they were killed."

The sale at Jefferson made the Slaughters rich men in poverty-stricken Reconstruction Texas. Grossing $24,300 for their share, the father and son partnership divided the funds, C. C.'s portion amounting to $8,100. In spite of their fortune, the North Texas cowmen still faced a major problem. Because the Texas frontier was full of ruthless men—army deserters, robbers, and vagrants—the Slaughters knew that their two-hundred-mile homeward trip would be very dangerous, and so they made careful preparations for their return. Realizing that wartime shortages had created a good market for manufactured goods on the isolated frontier, they converted part of their cash into new wagons, teams of oxen, groceries, men's clothing, boots, shoes, other dry goods, and oranges, "the first I ever saw," recalled Bill Slaughter.

Since the purchases amounted to only $4,000, the remainder of the money presented a problem. To prepare it for transporting, the Slaughters spread a wagon sheet on the ground and on it stacked twenty-dollar gold pieces in equal amounts. "Together father and C. C. rolled every stack tightly with wrapping paper and stuffed each roll into a pair of new leather saddlebags, to within a few inches of the top," Bill Slaughter remembered. "When the flaps were buckled down, C. C. threw them across my little pinto pony, back of my saddle, and father told me to mount up and head for home."

The Slaughter caravan then headed west, avoiding the main roads. A few miles from Palo Pinto, George and his sons left the wagon train, purportedly to visit a relative's ranch. Instead, they rode to within three miles of the village, where they cached their gold under a large boulder, rolled another stone over the entrance to the hiding place, put a mark on it, and then headed for home. Although mystified by his brother's and father's actions, Bill Slaughter later realized what their purpose was: "Banks were real curiosities in those days and I had no idea that C. C. was founding the first in our part of the country with that twenty thousand under that rock."

That financial reserve gave young C. C. Slaughter an opportunity to develop his business skills. He spread the word among his neighbors that he had made arrangements with "a bank in the East" whereby he could offer small amounts of gold for cattle. Short of specie, the ranchers responded, eagerly trading their oversupply of cattle for small amounts of the scarce gold. Obviously, Slaughter never told his neighbors that his "bank" was a cache under a rock and that the "East" was only three miles distant.[3]

C. C., with the aid of his father, also made a big profit on the mercantile goods purchased in Jefferson. Enlisting the labor and financial support of a Palo Pinto merchant, John A. McLaran, he established a general store. For five years the firm of McLaran and Slaughter was a leading mercantile house in the county. A principal factor behind its success was its barter for cattle. As many as seven hundred head per year were acquired through general store trading. Because people in the area had cattle but no money, such trade enabled the Slaughters to increase their cattle holdings.

The Slaughters' good fortune was not shared by many others in the cattle business. Kansas and Missouri continued to impose quarantines that blocked trail drives to important shipping points. A short corn crop in the Midwest forced farmers to market feeder cattle early, thereby driving down prices.

Late in 1867, however, the situation began to improve. Kansas relaxed its impositions against Texas cattle by opening a portion of the state to drovers. At the same time, the enterprising Joseph G. McCoy constructed shipping pens on the railroad at Abilene, Kansas, and sent circulars to every Texas cattleman whose address he could obtain. He also marked and posted the Chisholm Trail, thereby opening a new market for resourceful Texas ranchers. As a result about thirty-five thousand cattle were driven north out of Texas to Abilene in 1867.

When C. C. Slaughter learned of McCoy's shipping facilities in Abilene, he promptly convinced his father that they should send a herd north as soon as possible. In spite of the promise of large profits and ease of delivery offered by the Kansas promoter, the Slaughters approached the 1868 drive with cautious optimism. In addition to the natural dangers, especially floods and thunderstorms, they were also aware that Indians and outlaws could be an even more serious problem. Consequently, the Slaughters selected only eight hundred head for their first Kansas drive.

The Kansas drive, like that to Jefferson, was a family business operation. Both Bill and Peter accompanied trail boss C. C., who paid his younger brothers fifteen dollars a month. From Palo Pinto the Slaughters drove their cattle north to Jacksboro, then to Buffalo Springs in Clay County. There they turned east, followed the old California Emigrant's Trail twenty-one miles to Victoria Peak in Montague County near present-day Bowie, then pointed their herd in the direction of the North Star to Red River Station, twelve miles north of present-day Nocona and near the crossing on the Red River. There they struck the principal route of the Chisholm Trail. Averaging ten miles a day, they followed the Chisholm Trail across Indian Territory, entered Kansas near Caldwell, and completed the drive at Abilene without incident. Bill Slaughter's only noteworthy recollection of the trip was "an old fat merchant by the name of McClain who had a store made of cottonwood logs on the south side of the [Arkansas?] river with the sign on the South reading 'The Last Chance' to get supplies."[4]

At Abilene C. C. sold the cattle, which he had acquired for about seven dollars a head, to an Illinois buyer for forty-two dollars each. The combined profits from this sale and from the twelve hundred head sold that year to J. C. Loving, a neighbor and the son of the late Oliver Loving, netted the Slaughters almost forty thousand dollars.

Such profits convinced the Slaughter partners that their risks were justified. In 1869 George Webb and C. C., in two separate herds, drove two thousand head of cattle to Abilene. Having contracted for an early fall delivery, C. C. started north from Palo Pinto in late spring with the first herd. Near the Kansas border, he rode ahead to arrange the sale, leaving his younger brother Bill in charge. Soon after his departure, a party of Osage Indians intercepted the herd near present-day Kingfisher, but the younger Slaughter, after some delay, pacified the group with gifts, trail supplies, and cattle. Meanwhile, C. C. anxiously awaited the herd's arrival in Abilene. Several days passed. Finally, only three days before the contract was to expire, Bill arrived with the herd.

The second drive was already underway. Eager to profit from the excellent market, George Webb Slaughter decided to risk a fall trek. Disregarding the possibility of an early winter blizzard, he enlisted the aid of his son Pete and at least one of his neighbors. The community schoolteacher, J. H. Baker, also eager to share in the profits to be made in the cattle trade, joined the elder Slaughter. The combined herd numbered twelve hundred head.

The second drive left Palo Pinto on September 1, 1869. Averaging ten miles a day and slowed only by heavy rainstorms, the herd had reached the Arkansas River by October 1. In southern Kansas on the eighth, the Texans encountered other drovers who were holding more than twenty thousand cattle awaiting buyers. Unwilling to sell at the low prices offered, they turned their herd east to Walnut Creek valley near El Dorado, where they sold a portion to Kansas farmers.

A week later George Slaughter cut out five hundred head for winter pasture, to be sold the following spring, and sent the remainder to Abilene with Baker and Pete Slaughter. En route the drovers encountered C. C. Slaughter, who was returning from his earlier drive. Retracing his trail, C. C. accompanied his brother and Baker to Abilene, where he negotiated the sale of the cattle in this herd. The year's work grossed ninety thousand dollars. On December 1 the two Slaughter trail parties departed for home. Riding southward, the men were an impressive sight. Heavily armed, they rapidly traversed Indian Territory and by mid-December were back at their Palo Pinto homes, the first group having been gone for more than eight months.[5]

The 1869 drives virtually depleted the Slaughters of breeding stock. But because of the big demand for mercantile goods, they were able to acquire enough cattle through barter and purchase for another drive in 1870. That year the family drove three thousand cattle north, grossing $105,000, the highest return ever for the Slaughters. Such profits made the Slaughters (as well as many other Texas cattlemen) wealthy. In the early 1870s Kansas City banks showed cattle earnings of $3,000,000 annually, much of which was deposited to the credit of Texas drovers.

To maintain their profitable operation, the Slaughters made a number of adjustments. To control herds wintered in Kansas, George Webb, during the spring of 1870, moved with his wife and young children to Emporia, Kansas. There he was able to market the stock as it was driven north from Texas. Meanwhile, C. C. moved a herd from Texas to Indian Territory for wintering, and Pete and John remained on the home ranch at Palo Pinto. By the end of 1870, C. C. Slaughter had emerged as the dominant figure in the family operation. With approximately eight thousand cattle of his own and an additional four thousand held in partnership with his father, young Slaughter became the head of the business.

Profits from the trail-driving business, however, soon declined. Renewed Indian raids in North Texas disrupted Slaughter roundups and north-bound drives. On May 16, 1869, twelve cowboys, most of whom were employed by C. L. Carter, were attacked by a large party of Indians near the Slaughter Dillingham Prairie Ranch near Rock Creek in Young County. After a six-hour battle, the Indians withdrew, leaving three dead and five wounded. The following spring C. C.'s younger brother John was wounded at the Palo Pinto ranch when he surprised two Indians who were attempting to steal his horses. Although he lay incapacitated for six weeks, John fully recovered from the wound.

The next year, on April 19, 1871, George Slaughter, C. C., and twelve other men were similarly attacked by a raiding party in the same vicinity. Once under fire the elder Slaughter sent six men toward

Sand Creek with the cattle, while he and the others fortified themselves behind their horses. He then had some of the men slip away into a small ravine, where they could not be seen by the Indians, and open fire from another point. Thinking that reinforcements had arrived, the Indians retreated.

There were other raids that spring. A Slaughter trail herd was attacked at Victoria Peak in Montague County. While attempting to round up the scattered cattle, the Slaughter trail boss, a Mr. Adams, and a young cowboy were killed. John Slaughter assumed control of the herd and continued the northward drive. Near Lookout Mountain in Indian Territory, fifteen Comanches again stampeded the herd and drove off all the horses except those being ridden by the cowboys. In spite of the adversity, a remnant of the herd reached Abilene.

Meanwhile, on May 18 a large party of Kiowas, led by Satanta, attacked a federal government contract wagon train near Salt Creek in Young County, killing seven of its twelve teamsters. As a result of the Salt Creek Massacre, three of the Kiowa chiefs, Satanta, Big Tree, and Satank, were arrested at Fort Sill for the crime. Satanta and Big Tree (Satank was killed while trying to escape) stood trial at Jacksboro. This dramatic event, staged during the first two weeks of July 1871, heralded the beginning of the end of Indian depredations in Texas. Following recommendations by Indian agent Lawrie Tatum and Colonel Ranald S. Mackenzie that the United States Army be used to bring the Indians under control, General William T. Sherman sent troops into the field. For the next three years, the army methodically reduced the Comanches' and Kiowas' ability to attack frontier settlers. However, in spite of the army's work, the Slaughters were convinced that other adjustments in their operations were needed.

In June 1871 George and C. C. sold their cattle at Dillingham Prairie in Jack and Young counties to J. C. Loving and Charles Rivers for six dollars a head. C. C. took his pay in 1,065 head of feeder cattle and hired his brother Bill to drive them to an undisclosed leased pasture in Indian Territory. After wintering the herd there, C. C. marketed the fattened cattle in the spring of 1872 for a sizable profit.

Because winter feeding proved to be remunerative, the Slaughters decided to dispose of the remainder of their Palo Pinto cow herds in order to devote more attention to buying and selling cattle. On April 9, 1872, they sold all their cattle in Palo Pinto and adjoining counties for sixteen thousand dollars to M. P. Johnson, a Stephens County rancher. As the major partner, C. C. received fourteen thousand dollars, or seven-eights of the total sale. Apparently, however, Johnson defaulted on his note, and as a result C. C., in partnership with his brothers John and Bill, returned to Palo Pinto County in 1873, reobtained the Dillingham Prairie Ranch, and stocked it with improved cattle.[6]

For the next three years, the Slaughter operation remained basically a family affair. C. C. and his younger brothers continued to operate the Texas ranches and to supervise the trail drives. George Webb Slaughter remained in Kansas. In 1873 and 1874, the Slaughters sent two thousand head north each year, but the 1875 drive numbered only one thousand. Although they had grossed more than a quarter million dollars from trail driving, the family enterprise was dissolved in 1875. The Panic of 1873 and the extension of railroads to Dallas depressed range cattle prices. Fortunes earned by the drives to Kansas were wiped out overnight for those caught with large numbers of cattle. Prices fell from almost four cents per pound in early 1873 to one cent by November.

The market collapse also heralded a decline in the prominence of the rangy Texas longhorns. Even at depressed prices, corn-fed, well-bred cattle from northern feeders brought almost three times as much at the marketplace as Texas cattle. To meet such competition, Texas cattlemen began to look at new breeds of stock, at those requiring heavier investment. C. C. Slaughter, who in 1871 had begun selecting better quality Texas cows for his herd, did not immediately abandon the longhorn. Believing that by cross-breeding he could retain the range quality and, at the same time, obtain a more desirable beef quality animal, he sought to upgrade his herds by purchasing purebred stock. In 1874 he imported a number of shorthorn Durham bulls from Kentucky, one of the first Texas cattlemen to do so, and in September 1875 he bought twenty more shorthorn bulls. When the second shipment was herded through the streets of Fort Worth en route to Dillingham Prairie, the Fort Worth *Democrat* observed that the shorthorn would "soon be as familiar on the Texas prairies as the Longhorn is now." Within another year C. C. Slaughter had imported more than one hundred shorthorn bulls.

George Webb Slaughter briefly joined his son in the new investments. Returning to Texas, he and his family lived for a short time in Dallas but returned to the Palo Pinto ranch in 1875 after there was no longer any danger of Indian attack. There he built a twenty-five-thousand-dollar mansion in which he lived out his final twenty years. He retired from ranching in 1884 and died eleven years later. In 1875 the younger Slaughter brothers dissolved the partnership with their father and eldest brother. Peter Slaughter, however, continued to buy and sell cattle in partnership with his father until 1878. Peter then moved to West Texas and joined his brothers, John and Bill, who had established a ranch in Crosby County, fifty miles east of present-day Lubbock. In 1882 Peter moved his cattle from Texas to the Black River valley in Arizona, where he ranched until his death in 1911. John and Bill remained in Texas for a number of years.[7]

To attract other investors in the cattle business, C. C. Slaughter formed C. C. Slaughter and Company in 1873. Although the company was conceived to strengthen his cattle holdings, Slaughter soon found that he needed help from a banking friend to establish a sound financial base. After his own "banking" experience with the gold cache, he had done business with J. R. Couts, an enterprising Weatherford banker. Couts probably introduced Slaughter to William E. Hughes, a young Weatherford attorney. Through Hughes' influence, young C. C. Slaughter, trail driver, eventually became Colonel C. C. Slaughter, capitalist. Although C. C. Slaughter was never a colonel, his friends and acquaintances, in southern fashion, rewarded his rapid rise to wealth by referring to him by that title. In later years even his children referred to him as the Colonel.

Hughes was born in Illinois and in 1859 had moved to Texas. When the Civil War began, he returned to his native state briefly but slipped back into the South and served in the Confederate army. After Appomattox he returned to Texas, settling in the frontier village of Weatherford, thirty miles west of Fort Worth, where he taught school while completing study for admittance to the bar. From 1865 to 1873, he practiced law in Weatherford. His success in helping teamster Henry Warren recover losses incurred during the 1871 Salt Creek Massacre from the federal government won him a reputation as an excellent attorney.

C. C. Slaughter, Couts, and Hughes were examples of the new wealth of Texas—enterprising young men who took advantage of opportunities afforded by the South's struggling but resurging economy. Having long realized Texas' desperate need for capital, the three decided to pool their resources to establish a new banking venture. Rapidly growing Dallas seemed to offer the greatest promise.

In 1873 a Dallas newspaper heralded the city as "the commercial center of North Texas." The year before the former village had doubled its population to reach seven thousand residents. More than any other factor, the arrival that year of the Houston and Texas Central railroad, the city's first, caused the tremendous boom. Then in 1873 the Texas and Pacific Railway laid tracks from the east into the city, establishing important economic links in that direction. Dallas, at the crossroads of the two lines, virtually became the northern and western terminus of Texas. Merchants, shopmen, mechanics, speculators, and traders came from everywhere. The most conspicuous of these were the "terminus" storekeepers who followed the lengthening railroad from one new town to another. When they realized that the Houston and Texas Central was to go into Dallas, they bought seventy lots on Elm Street in one day.[8]

With the arrival of a second railroad in Dallas, the Texas and Pacific, Slaughter and his banking partners concluded that Dallas was the place to invest. On May 31, 1873, in league with an established insurance man, T. C. Jordan, Hughes, Slaughter, and Couts obtained a charter for the creation of a Dallas state bank to be capitalized at $250,000. From Weatherford, Hughes, Couts, and Slaughter secretly moved $42,000 in gold and silver in a buckboard across sixty miles of frontier roads to their new banking facilities in Dallas. Seventeen thousand dollars of the fund belonged to Hughes; C. C. Slaughter and J. R. Couts contributed $12,500 each. Named the City Bank of Dallas, the new business attracted investors. For a few months Slaughter, Couts, and Hughes remained in the background as directors. Jordan, who had practiced banking in connection with his insurance business, became the first president, and R. P. Aunspaugh was cashier.[9]

Despite the Panic of 1873, City Bank soon moved into a remodeled building, described by a newspaper as "an honor and ornament to Dallas." Financial troubles, however, forced President Jordan to sell his interest in the enterprise, and Hughes succeeded Jordan as president. C. C. Slaughter persuaded his father in 1874 to buy into the venture, and the elder Slaughter immediately moved from Kansas to booming Dallas to watch over his money.

C. C. Slaughter had already moved to Dallas. During October 1873 he had transported his family from Palo Pinto to "a mansion in the woods" and the "finest in the city," a new two-story frame house located on a twenty-acre tract on the northeast side of Dallas. Slaughter purchased the home from his banking partner, "Colonel" Hughes, for fifteen thousand dollars. True to his frontier background, Slaughter soon made his new homestead self-sufficient, complete with a large. garden, cows, chickens, fruit trees, and a cotton patch, which in 1880 produced five bales of cotton on twelve acres.

Slaughter's young family adapted rapidly to its new environment. Within two years Cynthia Jowell Slaughter had achieved a measure of prominence in Dallas society. Seemingly recovered from an 1873 illness, she became active in community activities. The five children, ranging in age from two to fourteen, kept busy with school and chores.

Tragedy, however, struck during the spring of 1876. In May, Cynthia became ill with what was termed a "complication of diseases." Though she gradually weakened, her illness for a time was not considered serious, but on May 16, while on business in Fort Worth, C. C. was suddenly called home to be with his wife. The following evening Cynthia died quietly in her sleep at the age of thirty-two. "Her sudden death was a terrible blow to the afflicted husband and five motherless children," reported the local newspaper, "and a large circle of friends [were] left to mourn her loss. Mrs. Slaughter was a most estimatable [*sic*] lady in all the relations of life, and her loss is a serious one to her family, her friends, and the community." [10]

Although grief-stricken, Slaughter soon sought a new mother for his children. While on a trail drive to Kansas during the summer of 1876—his last time to herd cattle north—Slaughter attended a church social in Emporia. According to family tradition, Slaughter asked some local Emporia residents to introduce him to a lovely young lady, but none did. Finally, he sought the help of the local Baptist preacher, A. M. Averill, a friend of Slaughter's father. Averill reluctantly agreed to introduce the bearded Texas cowman to the girl, who was Averill's twenty-four-year-old daughter, Carrie. When Slaughter returned to Texas, he coaxed a picture of Carrie from one of his younger sisters who had lived in Emporia.

In August, Slaughter wrote Carrie, requesting the pleasure of a correspondence with her. She curtly replied that "she was not in the habit of corresponding with strange men. . . . I am acquainted with a C. C. Slaughter of Dallas, Texas, but he is a married man and I would not consent to correspond with such a party," she wrote. "If you can see fit to let me know more fully who you are, and if connected with

G. W. Slaughter's family who used to reside here, I may consent to open a correspondence."

Slaughter quickly complied, explaining his wife's death. Soon the two were writing frequently. In mid-September Slaughter visited Carrie in Kansas, and late that month he requested her father's permission to ask Carrie to marry him. The Reverend A. M. Averill first asked Slaughter for credit references, then discreetly made several inquiries. In response R. G. Dun and Company of Dallas informed Averill that Slaughter was one of Dallas' leading citizens. "Mr. Slaughter is estimated worth from 80,000$ to 100,000$," and his "moral character above reproach. Commercially no one stands higher in this section."

With this information in hand, Averill allowed the courtship to progress rapidly. Wedding plans were announced in early November. But before final arrangements were made, Slaughter assured his future father-in-law that Carrie was to be in good hands and be a good mother. "No doubt we will find some thorns as we travel down life's uneven road," he wrote. "In regard to my children, . . . I believe her adequate to the task, no doubt she will make some mistakes, their own mother would do the same." In mid-January Slaughter returned to Kansas to claim his bride. At the Averill home in Emporia, after an all-night wedding party, he and Carrie Averill were married early in the morning of the seventeenth and immediately boarded a train for Dallas, Carrie's home until her death in 1928.[11]

Cynthia's death and C. C.'s marriage to Carrie Averill seemed to have little effect on Slaughter's business activities. During the summer of 1876, he increased his purebred stock by importing an additional one hundred shorthorn heifers from Kentucky. One-third of the new herd he drove to open range pastures in Mitchell County, on the frontier along the Colorado River near present-day Colorado City, and placed with a larger herd he had moved there from South Texas. The remainder of the improved breed he held at Dillingham Prairie Ranch in Jack County.

Although C. C. Slaughter's utilization of purebred cattle was at first a failure, it soon led to an important discovery. After the first season on the Slaughter pastures in Palo Pinto and Jack counties, the purebred Durham cattle began to die at an alarming rate. Slaughter diagnosed the disease as the dreaded Texas fever. Long a scourge for Kansas and Missouri after the appearance there of South Texas longhorns, the malady, for a reason then unknown to cattlemen, took a heavy toll of all other cattle wherever the longhorns had grazed.

Amazingly, the purebred cattle in Mitchell County were not affected. Slaughter did not know why but apparently concluded that pastures in far West Texas were safe from the disease, and he soon began seeking additional land there. "I did not know at this time it was the tick that caused the fever," he reflected twenty years later, "but I did know that they were even then accused of it. I made sure to take my cattle where I knew there were no ticks, moving away from them as they advanced, until I opened up ranches where they cannot come."

Until 1876 cattlemen had little opportunity to obtain large tracts of West Texas prairies. Most of the vast unsettled region west of the hundredth meridian was closed by natural and artificial barriers. For many years Comanche and Kiowa Indians roamed the prairies, frightening away any potential ranchers or settlers. Vast buffalo herds were also an obstruction to cattle raising. During the 1870s, however, both these barriers were eliminated. Following a large scale attack by Plains Indians on June 27, 1874, on a small party of buffalo hunters encamped at Adobe Walls on the Canadian River in the Texas Panhandle, the federal government dispatched five columns of troops into the region. In a strenuous and hazardous fall campaign, the army successfully routed the Indians from their traditional hunting grounds. After the surrender of Quahadi Comanche Chief Quanah Parker and his small band in June 1875, the Plains Indians no longer offered a barrier to white settlement in West Texas. Within another three years, buffalo hunters had virtually eliminated the shaggy beasts from the Texas Panhandle-Plains.

With the removal of Indians and buffalo, cattlemen faced little competition for use of the millions of acres of nutritious grass. Because of its semiarid climate, its treeless topography, and its isolation, western Texas offered little promise to prospective homesteaders; the farmers' frontier was not far enough advanced to move into the region. Only a few scattered sheepmen, most of whom were New Mexicans, grazed their flocks along the few running streams.

Likewise, only a few cattlemen rushed to take advantage of the excellent prairie grass because ranching there required a heavy investment. In addition to cattle costs, an open range operation required a maintenance crew of ten or more men, and necessary supplies had to be transported by wagon over hundreds of miles of poor or nonexistent roads. Furthermore, military and civil protection for life and property was minimal. Under such conditions only wealthy and enterprising capitalist-ranchers dared go there. Those who first took the risk were usually experienced cowmen who, already aware of the region's excellent suitability for ranching, formed partnerships with investors. Invariably, these men included former buffalo hunters, trail drivers, military scouts, or others who had seen firsthand the expansive prairies, sheltered canyons, and lush grasses. C. C. Slaughter's neighbor, Charles Goodnight, combining an investor's capital with his own intimate knowledge of the region, was the first cowman to penetrate the center of the Panhandle-Plains of Texas. He preceded Slaughter there by only one year.

With Oliver Loving, Goodnight had trailed cattle to Colorado following the Civil War, establishing the famous Goodnight-Loving Trail. In 1869 Goodnight settled in Pueblo, Colorado, and invested his trail-driving fortune in banking and in an ambitious water diversion project. During the Panic of 1873, his investments became worthless. Undaunted, he obtained a thirty thousand dollar loan from John Adair, an Irish capitalist, and reinvested in cattle. In 1875 he pastured his newly purchased herd along the Canadian River in northeastern New Mexico, and the following spring he moved eastward into Texas to the Llano Estacado, described as the "only uninhabitable portion of Texas."

Goodnight knew differently. As a military scout, he had visited Palo Duro Canyon, located on the headwaters of the Red River in the heart of the Panhandle. Remembering that the canyon and adjacent region was an ideal site for ranching, he returned in the summer of 1876 with his cattle and located in a park a thousand feet below where, two years before, Ranald S. Mackenzie's troops had surprised and routed Comanche, Kiowa, and Cheyenne Indians in the decisive battle of the Red River Indian War. There, in partnership with Adair, Goodnight established the famous JA Ranch. [12]

Apparently unaware of Goodnight's movements, C. C. Slaughter followed a similar pattern in his penetration of West Texas. In 1876, in partnership with South Texas cattleman John Scarborough, Slaughter moved two thousand head of cattle to the Colorado River near present-day Colorado City. Slaughter knew the range, having visited it with his father more than twenty years before. There he added to the herd, as previously noted, the shorthorn cattle. The following year Slaughter and Hughes purchased an interest in five thousand South Texas steers and heifers. In league with John Hullem, they moved this herd also to the Colorado valley, wintering the cattle at Renderbrook Springs, fifty-two miles north of present-day San Angelo.

A remnant of the Southern Plains formerly enormous buffalo herd briefly prevented Slaughter from moving his cattle farther northward up the Colorado River valley. During the summer of 1877, however, the last major segment of this herd was slaughtered by hunters only a few miles north of where Slaughter's cattle ranged, and in the spring of 1878, the survivors fled northward, never to return. [13]

Without the Indians and the buffalo, the valley of the Colorado was an ideal cattle range. Safe from tick fever, with adequate water and a mild climate, it provided Slaughter and his partners a vast expanse for ranching. To prevent others from laying claim first, Slaughter and Hughes immediately moved a herd of two thousand head from Palo Pinto. Apparently following a portion of the old Goodnight-Loving Trail, this herd, under the guidance of drover C. W. Foor, struck the Colorado River at present-day Colorado City. From there the cattle were moved upriver ten miles to the mouth of Deep Creek, where some were left to graze the lush mesquite grass; the remainder were driven to the head of Tobacco Creek, a tributary of the Colorado in Dawson County, nearly eighty miles northwest of where the Hullem cattle grazed. The sheltered valley along Tobacco Creek, known as Indian Canyon, lay between extensions of the Caprock which marked the southeastern extremity of the Llano Estacado. Between Tobacco Creek and the New Mexico border, seventy miles westward, there was no stream or body of fresh water.

During the spring of 1878, Slaughter and Hughes moved their Hullem cattle from Mitchell County fifty miles northwest to Rattle-snake Creek, a tributary of the Colorado in southern Borden County. Other cattle were purchased and placed along nearby Bull Creek. Branded HS, OS, O, and HU, the ten thousand head of cattle represented at least three different partnerships involving Slaughter. Then in May, to upgrade the herd, Slaughter added thirty purebred shorthorn bulls.

Slaughter's new venture into West Texas was more than an experiment in cattle raising. Prompted by heavy loss to his North Texas herds and tempted by the immediate availability of large tracts of land, he slowly relinquished his pastures in Palo Pinto and Jack counties. He fully realized the many risks involved in a move to West Texas. Renewed Indian outbreaks were quite possible. Since the new ranch lay nearly three hundred miles from a railroad or reliable transportation facilities, the maintenance of supply and communication lines would be costly. But he knew the country was well suited for the cattle industry, and he agreed wholeheartedly with an editorial in a South Texas newspaper concerning its potential: "With railroad facilities rapidly increasing by the extension of the Texas Pacific railway through the magnificent stock region lying between Fort Worth and El Paso, the business of cattle breeding must become one of great profit and national importance." Rising cattle prices, cheap land, and developing railroads would put an end to cattle trailing and give rise, in its stead, to an even bigger business—the breeding of fine herds. C. C. Slaughter was already taking steps for that transition.

Slaughter's expansion into West Texas culminated a decade of decisive action which reflected the entrepreneurial spirit then permeating the American West. His venture into cattle trailing, his use of family and neighbors as laborers, his establishment of a mercantile company and bank, his utilization of partnerships, his adoption of improved cattle breeds, and his relocation to new pastures were simply manipulations of an entrepreneur controlling factors of land, labor, capital, and available technology. Successful in his efforts, Slaughter joined the ranks of other businessmen-cattlemen who were then exploiting the West to their advantage. As had cattle barons John Wesley Iliff, Alexander Swan, Richard King, and George W. Littlefield, Slaughter had used the decade of the 1870s to build and enlarge his cattle domain. With his skills tested, he looked forward to the challenges of the 1880s.[14]

3

An Open Range Empire

Three men strolled out of the small ranch house. In quiet tones they discussed the dry weather and the alarming increases in cattle thefts. For nearly twenty years, the three veteran cowmen had been neighbors along the Brazos River breaks, together surviving Indian attacks, collapsed cattle markets, the Civil War, and other frontier misfortunes. Independently, each had accumulated a small fortune during the boom days of the cattle-trailing industry.

In the late fall of 1876, C. L. ("Kit") Carter and James C. Loving had ridden horseback several miles to pay more than a social visit to their neighbor, C. C. Slaughter, who was at his Dillingham Prairie Ranch to make an inspection of his Jack County cattle. Slaughter warmly welcomed his longtime friends whom he had rarely seen since he moved to Dallas. A war veteran who had accompanied Slaughter on the ill-fated venture to the Devil's River, one of the earliest settlers in Palo Pinto County, and a brother-in-law of Lawrence Sullivan Ross, Carter had fought in the Indian campaigns in North Texas. His son Shapley had been killed in a May 1869 raid along Rock Creek near Slaughter's ranch. Loving, a son of Oliver Loving and a partner of Charles Goodnight at the time of his death in 1867, had taken over his father's cattle-trailing business. Slaughter and Loving had traded in cattle for many years.

Adversity had once again drawn the three cowmen together. Although Indian attacks in North Texas had ceased, cattle rustling by white marauders had worsened. Nearby railheads made it easy for thieves to dispose of stolen cattle, and rising prices provided a lucrative return. Because of the unusually dry weather during the summer and fall of 1876, North Texas stockmen had scattered their herds for better forage over pastures too large to guard against theft. As a result of this combination of factors, cattle stealing had become intolerable.

Coincidentally, by 1876 the Texas cattle industry had begun to enjoy its greatest stability since the Civil War. The 1873 market collapse had driven many out of the industry, and increased trailing and shipping costs had forced survivors to become efficient business managers. Although the open range still prevailed, cattlemen could no longer recuperate their losses by rounding up mavericks. No longer were the North Texas prairies stocked with unclaimed longhorn cows and calves, and high-priced shorthorn cattle were being gradually replaced by the hardier native stock.

Perhaps a more subtle threat to their business had also drawn Carter, Loving, and Slaughter together. For many years these ranchers had relied upon the code of the open range—mutual respect for one another's range and water rights. Range boundaries were still delineated by nothing more than streams and hills. But in the wake of recovering economy, following the Panic of 1873 and the end of Indian depredations, thousands of settlers moved into the North Texas frontier and challenged the cattlemen's open range privileges. The population of the Palo Pinto–Young–Jack counties area, which numbered less than 1,000 in 1870, was annually increasing by 1,700 and by 1880 would total 17,237.

When the three cattlemen emerged from the Slaughter ranch house, they had decided to try to get all area stockmen to cooperate to solve their problems. They drafted a call, obtained the signatures of ten other cattlemen, and published a notice in the regional paper calling for all the cattlemen of Northwest Texas to meet at Graham on February 15, 1877, "for the purpose of determining the best method of gathering cattle and otherwise protecting the interest of all concerned."

On the appointed day, in response to the call, about forty men met at the courthouse in Graham and organized what eventually became one of the most powerful stock associations in the United States. C. C. Slaughter apparently did not attend the meeting but sent a representative. Called to order by J. N. Simpson of Parker County, the group, as its first order of business, elected Carter chairman and Loving secretary.

Bill Slaughter introduced a resolution proposing that the convention outline its objectives and purposes, and Carter responded by appointing a committee of seventeen that included John N. Simpson, J. C. Loving, Bill Slaughter, Joseph Graham, and D. B. Gardner, who later became manager of the famed Pitchfork Ranch.

The committee completed a draft of resolutions late that night. On the morning of the sixteenth, the resolutions were read to the assembled cattlemen. The preamble called upon the ranchers to "work together for the good and common interest of the Stock Raisers of Northwestern Texas, and to do all in their powers for the promotion of the stock interests." One resolution provided for the division of the North Texas cattle country into six districts for the purpose of conducting cooperative roundups. District I included the Slaughter ranching interests.

Other resolutions suggested solutions to common problems. One proposed that, when removing a herd from a range, the owner or manager of the company must give notice to three nearby stockmen within the district and authorize them to examine the herd. All the animals found by examiners to belong to others the rancher was to "cut out and hold the same and give the owner thereof notice at the earliest practical moment." The most important resolutions sought to deal with blatant theft of cattle, "intentional or otherwise," by preventing stockmen from selling their neighbor's cattle without permission. The cattlemen's convention approved the resolution and adjourned, having laid the foundation for the Northwest Texas Cattle Raisers Association, which eventually became the Texas and Southwestern Cattle Raisers Association. Although Slaughter limited his participation in the association for several years, his name is firmly linked with its founding. His close friends, Loving and Carter, were elected its first officers, and his desires were presented in a resolution to the convention through his brother Bill.[1]

The organization, designed to accommodate established North Texas cattlemen, afforded C. C. Slaughter excellent opportunities. Because it provided for cooperative roundups and antitheft measures and its jurisdiction encompassed Palo Pinto, Jack, Young, and other counties to the west, the organization meant that Slaughter and the other major ranchers could operate with fewer men and less risk and thus could expand westward. As a result Slaughter increasingly devoted more time to his newly established Long S Ranch, the second largest ever in West Texas.

By 1878 the Long S had begun to take definite shape. Situated along fifty miles of the Colorado, its range included the rolling breaks of four live-water tributaries, Bull, Rattlesnake, Tobacco, and Sulphur creeks. The ranch's eastern border lay in the shadow of Muchakooaga [Muchaque] Peak in Borden County, long a distinct landmark and rendezvous point for nomadic Indians and Comancheros. To the northwest the ranch's prairie gave way to the sharp rise of the Caprock Escarpment that divided the rolling plains from the level Llano Estacado. Because he was among the first to push his cattle to the unclaimed lands above the Caprock, Slaughter, in accordance with the code of the open range, was able to claim as much land as he wanted. Before long his stock were ranging over much of Howard, Martin, Dawson, Borden, and Gaines counties, or from present-day Gail and Stanton on the east to Seminole on the west and from approximately ten miles north of Big Spring and Midland on the south to Indian Springs, northeast of Lamesa, on the north. The rangeland included Cedar Lake in northern Gaines County. Longtime Slaughter cowboy Jack Alley estimated the boundaries to be about forty by eighty miles, a size second only to the vast XIT Ranch. On the other hand, C. W. Foor, who accompanied the Slaughter herd from Palo Pinto to the Colorado, estimated the range to be about fifty miles "north to south and the same distance east to west. Our cattle ranged west through the Plum Creek country [southwest Borden County] and clear down to the Big Spring. We located a camp on Bull Creek, about 20 or 25 miles west of headquarters [Deep Creek camp], and a camp on Morgan Creek [eastern Howard County] about fifteen miles south of the headquarters. We had a camp at German Springs [southern Borden County] to catch the heavy drifts and also a camp at Rattlesnake Springs [southern Borden County]. Our cattle ranged clear up to the Colorado. We called it fifty miles from the headquarters of the ranch to the headwaters of the river. Our ranch ran from Muchaway [Muchakooaga] Peak [Borden County] to Big Springs."[2]

Apparently by design, Slaughter's new ranch lay directly in the path of the proposed Texas and Pacific railroad route.[3] And although virtually waterless, the adjacent High Plains afforded excellent summer pastures. Temporary headquarters for the sprawling ranch was first at the mouth of Bull Creek, near some old rock corrals thirteen miles southwest of present-day Snyder in Scurry County. Concluding that the pens had been abandoned, Slaughter and his partners made immediate use of them. A hole dug in a clay bank and covered with mesquite poles and dirt was the first ranch house. A dried bullhide hanging from the rafters by the tail served as the door. Although primitive, the site had been occupied the previous year by two other cattlemen. To Slaughter's surprise the initial claimants were his younger brothers, John and Bill, who returned with cattle in 1877. "A little matter of this kind caused no hard feelings between the brothers, for there was so much land left," reported Jack Alley, an observer of the scene. The younger brothers thereupon drove their cattle north another hundred miles to Blanco Canyon in Crosby County.

Although their cattle were three hundred miles from a railroad, Slaughter and his partners visited the ranch as often as possible. During the spring of 1878, Slaughter and Hughes, accompanied by a Negro cook, drove from Dallas to the ranch in a hack pulled by a team of fine matched mules. From Dallas to Fort Griffin, the cattlemen followed established stage roads by way of Fort Worth and Weatherford. At Fort Griffin they turned west-southwest, following a little used but established trail through central Jones and Fisher counties (approximately the route of U.S. Highway 180). Their road carried them into southern Scurry County near present-day Hermleigh to their ranch headquarters on the Colorado.

Although the trip was uneventful, a party of Indians who had slipped from the reservation in Indian Territory created some excitement for the Dallas bankers. Under cover of darkness, the Indians slipped into the unsuspecting camp during the roundup and stole the cowboys' saddle horses and Slaughter's mule team. Left afoot, the two businessmen had to take two work oxen from the ranch to pull their wagon.

The return trip took ten days to Fort Griffin, where the cattlemen had to deal with a new difficulty. "The hack seat was pretty hard and the constant exposure finally wore the seat of Hughes' trousers out," Alley remembered. "Hughes was a fastidious dresser, and when they got within a few miles of Fort Griffin, he hid in the brush while Colonel Slaughter went into town for a new pair of trousers."

The inconvenience did little to discourage the West Texas venture. In 1878 Slaughter and Hughes purchased Hullem's interest in the cat-

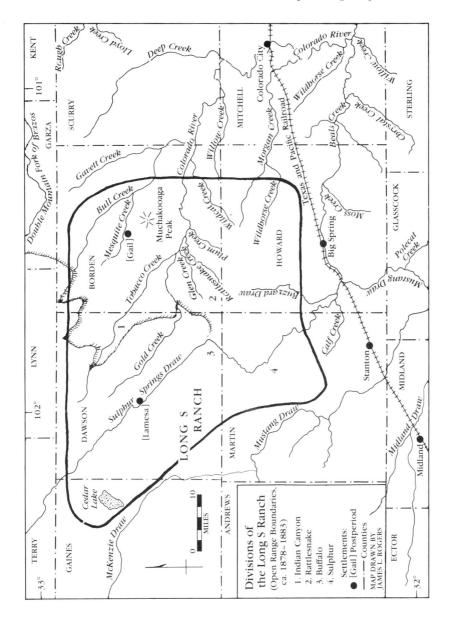

Divisions of
the Long S Ranch
(Open Range Boundaries,
ca. 1878–1883)

1. Indian Canyon
2. Rattlesnake
3. Buffalo
4. Sulphur

Settlements:
● [Gail] Postperiod
    — — Counties

MAP DRAWN BY
JAMES L. ROGERS

tle. Profits were insured by an excellent calf crop, adequate rainfall, and an absence of Indian threat. However, in 1879 Slaughter and Hughes decided to divide their banking and cattle partnership. Hughes wanted to develop his own ranch, and Slaughter had the greater investment along the Colorado. A simple division was effected; Slaughter traded his interest in the City Bank of Dallas for Hughes' share of the cattle.[4]

For the first time in his life, C. C. Slaughter was in the cattle business without a partner. No longer did he need the financial and physical support previously supplied by his father, brothers, or banking partners. With virtually unlimited grass, adequate water, and a fine herd of ten thousand cattle, he was now in a position to ranch as he pleased. And as his leases expired in Jack and Young counties, he consolidated his holdings along the Colorado tributaries.

The 1880 calf crop bore a new brand. To replace the multitude of other marks acquired in the various partnerships, Slaughter devised a brand that was representative of his name and his immense ranch. Henceforth, on the left side of all his cattle he placed an elongated reclining S (⌒). The 2,400 square miles of West Texas where his cattle grazed was known simply as "Slaughter country." The new Long S Ranch was firmly established.

Slaughter immediately began to improve his new domain. In 1881 he moved the headquarters from Bull Creek westward to German Springs, twenty miles north of Big Spring. The new site, more centrally located, afforded better access to the newly completed Texas and Pacific railroad. The scattered sheepherder dugouts, which had been used as the camp's first dwellings, were replaced with a long box house. Constructed with a wide hall in the center and a full-length porch on the front, this building served as the ranch's headquarters for the next twenty years.

Slaughter separated the ranch into four divisions. German Springs, the main headquarters, served as headquarters of the Rattlesnake division, a large pasture bordering Rattlesnake and Plum creeks in southwestern Borden County. Indian Springs, ten miles east of present-day Lamesa, became headquarters for the Tobacco Creek division. At this site a small frame house was the home of a cowboy and his wife. This division encompassed the eastern half of Dawson County and a small portion of northwestern Borden County. Fifteen miles south of Lamesa, at a large spring near the Dawson-Martin county line, Slaughter had erected a large frame house to serve as headquarters for the Buffalo division. Obtained from the Buffalo Sheep Company, this range extended north along Sulphur Draw and encompassed the southern portion of Dawson County. The Sulphur division, watered by a large spring on Sulphur Draw twenty miles north of present-day Stanton, lay south of the Buffalo division and encompassed most of eastern Martin County. Sulphur Springs, a well-used watering site on the Fort Worth—El Paso trail, was at the center of the division.

For several years Slaughter maintained complete control of his four open range divisions. Because he had occupied the principal water supply in each, no competitor could effectively intrude. By means of leases and purchases of small tracts, he operated without fence or without having to purchase any large acreage. State land was leased for as little as three cents an acre. And because the major part of his ranch lay within the bounds of the Texas and Pacific railroad grant, Slaughter was able to use the state's alternate sections without cost by leasing the other alternate sections from the railroad. Thus, almost uncontested, Slaughter controlled an area of West Texas encompassing more than 1,500,000 acres, an area twice the size of the state of Rhode Island.[5]

By 1882 the cattle industry in West Texas was booming. Rising cattle prices inspired a wave of South and East Texas cattlemen to seek a site for a "beef bonanza" on the West Texas Plains. Between 1878 and 1882, the Spade, XIT, T-Anchor, Mill Iron, Shoe Bar, Frying Pan, Quarter Circle Heart, LS, and Diamond F ranches were established in the region north of Slaughter's Long S. Then as the result of reports in eastern and British newspapers on the lucrative American range cattle industry, eastern and British capitalists moved in. By 1883 eighteen major companies had been created in Scotland and England for investment in American cattle ranches. Some of these and others obtained range privileges and acquired title to land in western Texas. New ranches in the Panhandle and South Plains included the Scottish-owned Matador Land and Cattle Company, Limited, the Francklyn Land and Cattle Company, the St. Louis Cattle Company, the Pitchfork Land and Cattle Company, and the Kentucky Cattle Raising Company.

The influx of capital led to inflated prices. Slaughter, like several other pioneer cattlemen, was tempted to sell out for high profits. In 1881 he was approached by two English investors who offered him a half million dollars for his West Texas ranch interests. Without much deliberation, Slaughter accepted the offer. The Englishmen left for

West Texas after getting an order from Slaughter instructing the foreman to turn the ranch over to them. Three days later Slaughter learned
the buyers did not have the money. To block the transfer, he dispatched his ten-year-old son, Bob, by horseback to warn the ranch
foreman. Using three horses and without rest, Bob made his legendary
"half-million dollar ride," more than three hundred miles, in forty-one
hours to the German Springs headquarters, arriving there ahead of the
Englishmen.[6]

The Long S brand soon gained nationwide attention. From Colorado City in 1882, Slaughter shipped the best of his improved crossbred cattle on the Texas and Pacific Railway line. For this shipment he
loaded 350 head of three-year-old Durham-longhorn steers on eleven
cars, personally rode with them to St. Louis, and sold the lot for seven
cents a pound, reportedly the highest price paid for grass-fed beef to
that date. The steers averaged 1,090 pounds per head, even after six
days in transit, and grossed nearly $27,000. The sale attracted nation-
wide attention, and henceforth Slaughter was increasingly referred to
as the "Cattle King of Texas."

The sale also invited prospective investors to his door. During the
summer of 1882, Slaughter was approached by another English group
who offered him one million dollars for his West Texas holdings. He
declined. The cost of establishing a new ranch would be excessive, and
the five to ten thousand calves produced each year provided unpar-
alleled returns on his investment.

His large profits and the growing competition for rangeland convinced Slaughter that he needed to insure permanent control of his
West Texas domain. Despite the growing public opposition to ownership of large amounts of land by cattlemen, he set out to acquire as
much as possible. "I began to buy [additional] land with the profit
[from the 1882 sale]," Slaughter testified many years later. "[The high
cattle prices] gave me a big start and from that time on I kept moving
on."

The invention of barbed wire, the extension of the Texas and
Pacific railroad into West Texas, and competition for grazing land
spurred Slaughter to enclose portions of his range. Barbed wire, in-
vented in 1874, enabled cattlemen to construct crude, inexpensive
fences capable of holding large and small cattle alike; the railroad provided cheap transportation of posts and wire to within twenty miles of
the ranch; and high prices for cattle increased competition for grass. As

a result Slaughter invested heavily in fencing. His first fence, probably constructed in 1883, was primarily a drift fence to keep cattle from encroaching on Slaughter grass. It extended from fifteen miles south of Gail, in Borden County, north and west to the Lynn County line, fifteen miles south of Tahoka.

Wire and posts for Slaughter's fencing were freighted from Colorado City or Big Spring. Posts cost ten cents; wire, fifteen cents per pound; and labor, ten cents a rod. Construction costs were approximately $250 per mile. By mid-1885 Slaughter had built about one hundred miles of fence at a cost of $25,000.

Even though the range was partially fenced, more than eighty men were required for the ranch's semiannual roundups. These events, staged in May and September, were planned cooperatively through the auspices of the Clear Fork and Colorado cattlemen's association. Large roundups were typical for Slaughter in the early 1880s. He retained most of his 1882 calf crop, and as a result his herd at the end of that year numbered forty thousand head. Annual calf production had reached twelve thousand.

With such increase Slaughter sought to expand his million-acre holdings. In 1884 he entered into two separate partnerships, thereby getting access to an additional 700,000 acres. In one of the partnerships, early that year, he acquired half interest in a large ranch fifteen miles west of present-day Plainview. There in 1881 T. W. and J. N. Morrison had purchased 81,000 acres along both sides of Running Water Draw in the corners of Lamb, Hale, Swisher, and Castro counties. An additional 100,000 acres of school land were available in the alternate sections. Extending from South Tule Draw west to near present-day Dimmitt and south to Hart's Camp near Olton, the ranch was the only one on the High Plains between the vast XIT on the west and Charles Goodnight's JA to the northeast. Its headquarters was on the south side of Running Water Draw, seventeen miles northwest of Plainview. The Morrisons sold a portion of their interest in their Cross L Ranch to Iowa financier W. D. Johnson and stocked the remainder with three thousand head. Needing additional cattle, J. N. Morrison negotiated a partnership whereby Slaughter traded three thousand head of Long S cattle for half interest in the ranch.

For Slaughter it was an excellent deal. Not only did it give him half interest in six thousand cattle and access to 181,000 acres, but it also brought immediate relief to his overstocked Long S. "It was mighty

bleak open country and not much protection," remembered Rufe
O'Keefe, a Slaughter cowboy who drove the cattle to the new ranch,
but "it was the best grass [I] had seen lately . . . compared to that Big
Springs [*sic*] country where I had just come from." The first cattle in
the new partnership were branded with a circle; for several years the
ranch bore the name Circle and was eventually stocked with twenty
thousand head of cattle.⁷

In 1884 Slaughter entered into an even larger venture when he
obtained a partnership with R. D. Hunter and A. G. Evans in a one-
million-acre lease on the Cheyenne-Arapaho Reservation in Indian Territory. He had done business with Hunter for many years. A Texas
cowman, Hunter in 1873 had established a livestock commission business in Kansas City. There, while at market, Slaughter became acquainted with Hunter and in 1877 sold him cattle to be grazed on the
Cheyenne-Arapaho Reservation. Successful in his venture on Indian
lands, Hunter worked tirelessly to obtain additional leases. Finally,
after the Department of the Interior had reduced Cheyenne-Arapaho
beef rations in 1882, the Indians requested through their agent that a
few herds of cattle be permitted in the remote portions of their reservation with the lease proceeds designated to supplement beef rations. On
December 12, 1882, a council of Cheyenne and Arapaho chiefs approved the leasing policy, charging two cents per acre, half to be paid
in breeding stock and the remainder in money.

Among the first lessees were Hunter and Evans, each of whom had
obtained 500,000 acres. Granted permission in January 1883 by agent
John D. Miles and the chiefs to stock the leases, the partners invited
several cattlemen to enter into partnerships. C. C. Slaughter accepted
their invitation by selling them a two-thirds interest in eight thousand
two- and three-year-old steers.⁸

By April 1, 1884, cattle from the Long S were en route for Indian
Territory. Divided into three herds, they were trailed east from Tobacco
Creek by way of present-day Snyder and the Pease River valley to a
point near Vernon. The herds passed near the site where Slaughter had
witnessed the rescue of Cynthia Ann Parker twenty-three years before.

At Doan's Crossing on the Red River, the Slaughter cowboys turned
the cattle north. Following the Great Western (Dodge City) Trail across
the Red River, the drovers moved the herds northeast across the Kiowa-
Comanche Reservation to the Hunter and Evans leases, about forty
miles northwest of Fort Reno. There, under the supervision of Slaugh-

ter's superintendent, G. W. Wolfe, the cattle grazed on pastures of bluestem grasses six to eight inches tall, described by Long S cowboy Rufe O'Keefe as "the finest grass I ever saw."

As a result of the new partnership, Slaughter now had available nearly 1,500,000 acres of grass and cattle spread from the South Plains of Texas deep into Indian Territory. With such extensive holdings, he logically became a major leader in southwestern cattle activities and associations.

In February 1880 Slaughter joined his neighboring cattlemen along the Brazos and Colorado rivers in forming the Stock Raisers Association of the Clear Fork and Colorado. Meeting at Buffalo Gap, south of Abilene, on February 23, 1880, the group called "for the better protection of our stock interests" and patterned its organization after the three-year-old Northwest Texas Stock Raisers Association. Influenced especially by Slaughter and C. L. Carter, the Clear Fork and Colorado cattlemen established five roundup districts. The association named Slaughter to the first executive committee.

The association met twice yearly to determine rules, time, meeting place, and superintendent for the roundup in each district. Each participating ranch supplied a wagon and from five to ten men. Each man was allowed six horses, but was instructed to "leave all race horses at home." And at the 1885 roundup, the superintendent was given authority to discharge "any man who introduces card playing in any outfit."[9]

In May 1884 one of the largest roundups ever held in Texas was made. Fifteen thousand Slaughter cattle were gathered in a pasture one-half mile square. Work crews from all area ranches gathered on the Slaughter ranch. The elected roundup boss then divided the men into groups and ordered each one to make a dry camp ten miles away, each in a different direction "like the spokes of a wheel." At sunup each group fanned out to contact the wing of the others on each side, then all proceeded to drive cattle toward the center of the twenty-mile circle. The scene made a vivid impression on Slaughter's young son Bob. "By ten A.M. fifteen thousand head were milling in the flat," he recalled. "All through the long afternoon the cutting kept on until our number had finished in the afterglow of a western sunset. I'll say it was some roundup."

Slaughter also remained active in the Northwest Texas Stock Raisers Association. At its fourth annual convention at Jacksboro, March

8–9, 1880, he was appointed to the spring and fall roundup committee by president C. L. Carter. Evidently very popular among his peers, he was "loudly called for" to address the convention. As recorded by secretary J. C. Loving, Slaughter "responded in his usual easy way with a lengthy speech." He recounted the history of cattle raising in North Texas and the many disadvantages, "troubles," and losses incurred in ranching. The association had brought about many wonderful benefits to the region, Slaughter continued, and he urged its members to continue the good work. "I lived and worked in this country when, if we got our cattle or any cattle, we had to 'go for 'em,' and we did it. Often we did not get them. . . . That day, thanks to this association, has passed." He also urged members to work for lower rail rates. According to Loving, "His whole speech was received with enthusiasm by the entire audience as was evidenced by the applause."

At the March 14–16, 1881, convention at Fort Griffin, Slaughter was reappointed to the roundup committee, was nominated as first vice-president, and was named to a special committee charged with drafting resolutions protesting pending legislation which threatened ranchers' free use of public domain. At the March 20–22, 1882, convention at Gainesville, he was appointed to the committee on resolutions and finance. As a member of that committee, he was largely responsible for a proposal that a protective and detective committee be formed to employ inspectors to watch shipping points, feed and butcher pens, and herds moving throughout the bounds of the association. Adopted by the convention, the resolution marked the beginning of the association's inspection process.

Slaughter became an ardent supporter of the detective system. At the March 6–8, 1883, convention in Fort Worth, he insisted that what was needed to make the association an effective body against lawlessness was "less laws and more money." In a stirring speech, he told the cattlemen that he would favor a "tax on stock" so that funds could be raised to employ cattle inspectors. "Put enough men and enough money around cattle," he said, "and you protect them." Slaughter's speech not only assured the passage of such a resolution, but also got him on a committee for the reorganization of the association and on its prestigious executive committee. Then in May the executive committee appointed him chief of inspectors and detectives.

Slaughter chose several deputies to watch pens and shipping points. In his annual report to the 1884 convention, he stated that his inspec-

C. C. Slaughter, ca. 1876. Photo courtesy of the Southwest Collection, Texas Tech University.

George Webb Slaughter,
ca. 1893. Photo courtesy of
the Southwest Collection,
Texas Tech University.

(Left to right): Minnie Slaughter Veal, Florence (Mrs. R. L.) Slaughter,
Dela Slaughter Wright, and Allie (Mrs. George) Slaughter. Ca. 1894.
Photo courtesy of the Southwest Collection, Texas Tech University.

Cynthia Jowell Slaughter (left). Carrie Averill, ca. 1876 (above). Photos courtesy of the Southwest Collection, Texas Tech University.

(Front, left to right): Carrie Slaughter, unidentified, unidentified, C. C. Slaughter, Florence (Mrs. R. L.) Slaughter, Elma (Mrs. C. C.) Slaughter, and George Veal; (back, left to right): Minnie Slaughter Veal and R. L. ("Bob") Slaughter. Ca. 1900. Photo courtesy of the Southwest Collection, Texas Tech University.

Lazy S headquarters, ca. 1899. This site was probably two miles southwest of present-day Morton in Cochran County. Photo courtesy of the
Southwest Collection, Texas Tech University.

Long S roundup, ca. 1900, with the Slaughter family participating.
Photo courtesy of the Southwest Collection, Texas Tech University.

C. C. Slaughter (left) and George Slaughter mounted for a roundup, ca. 1900. Photo courtesy of the Southwest Collection, Texas Tech University.

Lazy S headquarters, constructed in 1915. From the painting *Adobe Headquarters* by Mondel Rogers, in the collection of Nancy M. O'Neil. Used by permission. Photo courtesy of the Baker Gallery of Fine Art, Lubbock, Texas.

C. C. Slaughter (right) and T. F. B. Sotham with Sir Bredwell following the 1899 purchase.

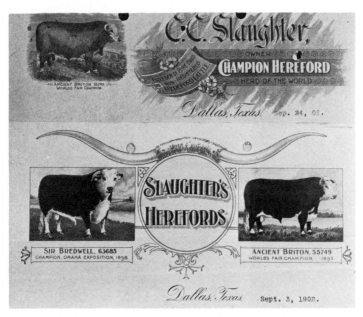

C. C. Slaughter's letterheads, designed to promote his Hereford cattle. From the George M. Slaughter Papers, Southwest Collection, Texas Tech University.

Panhandle Stockmen's Association, Roswell, New Mexico, 1907. George Slaughter (standing) delivers the welcoming address. C. C. Slaughter is seated at center stage. Photo courtesy of the Southwest Collection, Texas Tech University.

C. C. Slaughter (in cupola) poses with his children and grandchildren at the Slaughter mansion, ca. 1902. Photo courtesy of the Southwest Collection, Texas Tech University.

The Slaughter family in 1905. Pictured with their children and grandchildren are Colonel and Mrs. C. C. Slaughter (seated). The small boy at
left is Jo Dick Slaughter. Seated on the ground is Ed Dela Wright. In
the first row (standing, left to right) are Roberta Wright, Minnie
Slaughter Veal, Nelle Slaughter, Stuart Wright, Dela Slaughter Wright,
R. L. Slaughter, Jr., and Gilbert Wright (in uniform). In the second
row are Allie (Mrs. George) Slaughter with baby Eloise, Carrie (Mrs. E.
Dick) Slaughter, C. C. Slaughter, Jr., Elma (Mrs. C. C.) Slaughter, Jr.,
G. G. Wright, Florence (Mrs. R. L.) Slaughter, Dr. George Veal, Alex
Slaughter, Carrie Slaughter Dean, Dr. John Dean, and George Slaughter
II (on rail). At left on the rail is Jowell Wright. At back left are Bob,
George, and E. Dick Slaughter. Photo courtesy of the Southwest Collec-
tion, Texas Tech University.

tors had checked 970,000 head at trails and markets, had caught and saved 500 head of association members' cattle, and had "good cause to believe that they had saved many more hundreds or probably thousands of cattle that would have been illegally taken from the owners had it not been for the fact they . . . were keeping watch at the markets."

Slaughter's growing influence on the Northwest Texas Stock Raisers Association was evident in another area. At the 1882 conference in Gainesville, he began promoting Dallas as a future convention site, an unlikely choice since the association's jurisdiction lay in a region sixty miles or more from the city. Slaughter's plea was rejected, but his words did not go unheeded. At the 1883 convention in Fort Worth, he renewed his invitation, and Dallas was selected for the 1884 convention "by acclamation and loud applause." Secretary Loving recorded that "Colonel Slaughter is promising to Set 'em up lively when the Cow-men come." Slaughter did not disappoint his friends. The Dallas convention, held March 11–13, 1884, attracted five hundred cattle raisers and guests and was highlighted by an elaborate banquet and ball, "complete with ten electric lights" and "G. H. Mumm's extra dry [whiskey], bottled and labeled 'expressly for the Texas Stockmen's Convention.'"[10]

At the March 10–12, 1885, convention in Sherman, cattlemen paid Slaughter a high honor. When Carter unexpectedly announced his retirement, Slaughter and two others were nominated for president. The other two withdrew their names, and Slaughter was elected unanimously. Editor George B. Loving of the *Texas Livestock Journal* was highly pleased with the choice. "The members of the N.W.T.C.R.A. did honor to themselves and this organization. No man has done more for the cattle interests of Texas and there is no man who will do more for the same great industry in the future."

As president, Slaughter presided over the tenth annual session of the association at its March 10, 1886, convention at Weatherford. During its short history, attendance had grown from forty at the first meeting at Graham to more than five hundred at Weatherford. In opening the convention, Slaughter added a new feature by having a prayer offered by a local pastor, unique because, as Slaughter told an interviewer a week later, "praying cattlemen are the exception and not the rule in Texas."

When he was nominated at Weatherford for a second term, Slaughter declined to serve. In what was called an eloquent speech, he told the convention that C. L. Carter had served with great ability for nine years and deserved to be president again. Slaughter, however, remained one of the association's favorite speakers. Following the March 7, 1887, convention in Fort Worth, a local reporter remarked, "For a man who shoots from the shoulder, C. C. Slaughter is a crack marksman."

Slaughter's ascendancy in the Northwest Texas Cattle Raisers Association closely paralleled the development of his West Texas cattle empire. During the decade following 1876, he had consolidated his holdings, developed one of the largest single-unit ranches in West Texas, abandoned the ancient open range system in favor of enclosure, and expanded into the Panhandle and Indian Territory. Such success did not go unnoticed by his peers.

He also enjoyed an excellent reputation among the cowboys who worked for him. His punctual payment of wages in cash, supplemented with a steady supply of "the best food" available, created continuing loyalty among his hired men. Consequently, cowboys worked on his ranches for ten years or longer; one man, Jack Alley, was a Slaughter employee for nearly forty years.[11] And when Long S cowboys gathered around a camp fire at night, Slaughter's jovial personality, humorous wit, interesting tales about frontier days, and intimate knowledge of the cattle business further enhanced his popularity.

Slaughter's reputation as a great cattleman was strengthened by his success in banking. Although he had disposed of his interests in the City Bank of Dallas in 1879, when he and W. E. Hughes had dissolved partnership, he reinvested in that bank in 1881, when it reorganized as City National Bank. As its vice-president, Slaughter restricted his role primarily to soliciting the business of "stock raisers and Western merchants."

Because of the rapid growth of Dallas, Slaughter was convinced that the city could support still another bank, even though it already had five. Thus, in March 1884, in partnership with the private banking firm of Thomas and Gannon, he obtained a charter for the American National Bank. Established with a paid-in capital of $200,000 and with an authorized capital of $500,000, Slaughter assumed the post of vice-president, a position he would hold until his death. W. H. Thomas was the first president, and W. J. Gannon its first cashier.[12]

Slaughter enjoyed his role as a distinguished banker-cattleman. He was a short heavyset man with a neatly trimmed beard and usually was seen holding a small cigar. He mingled easily with both Dallas society and West Texas cowboys. Greatly influenced by the graceful manners of his former partner W. E. Hughes, the once quick-tempered Slaughter had become a man of national stature. He was a famous cattleman, he was president of one of the largest regional stock associations, he was owner or had under lease immense areas of land, he was owner of perhaps more cattle than any other single individual in Texas, and he was a prominent banker. The future appeared bright, but for Slaughter, and the western cattle industry in general, dark days lay ahead. The fact that C. C. Slaughter was able to survive drought and depression during the next decade was an even greater success story than that of the previous ten years.

4

Survival of
the Fittest

Until 1885 cattlemen in West Texas enjoyed an almost ideal situation. A free range, freedom from Indian raids and from taxation, favorable weather conditions, and constantly rising prices allowed most to prosper. Because it was far from the line of permanent settlement, the thriving cattle business in West Texas operated with little interference from two traditional opponents, farmers and town promoters. Thus, it is no wonder that the era was known as the "beef bonanza."

The West Texas situation was duplicated throughout the Great Plains. In Colorado, John Wesley Iliff built a herd of 40,000 head that ranged over a 150-mile area along the South Platte River. Alexander Swan established a similar empire in Wyoming with herds approaching 120,000. Like C. C. Slaughter and other cattlemen on the Southern Plains, they enjoyed handsome profits. [1]

Contributing to the cattle bonanza in Texas was the state's generous land policy. On July 14, 1879, the legislature passed a law, designed to generate revenue, providing for the sale of unappropriated nonschool lands in fifty-four West Texas counties for fifty cents an acre. And under the provisions of the Constitution of 1876, railroads were granted up to sixteen sections of land for every mile of rail construction. The Texas and Pacific received for its 994 miles of road 5,173,120 acres, most of which lay in West Texas. Because he had located the Long S within the boundaries of the Texas and Pacific survey, C. C. Slaughter perpetuated his hold on a vast tract of West Texas land by securing from the Texas and Pacific in 1881 a five-year lease of 192,000 acres, primarily in the four corners of Dawson, Howard, Martin, and Borden counties. This land included a corresponding amount of public school land which Slaughter used free until 1882.

In November of that year, however, a farmer-oriented Texas legislature sought to end the cattlemen's free use of state land. West Texas stockmen responded through the newly created Texas Livestock Association. C. C. Slaughter and others pressured the legislature to enact a law that would allow cattlemen to lease large blocks of land for ten to twenty years at a minimal price. Although he was unable to attend the association's initial meeting in Austin in February 1883, Slaughter sent chairman George B. Loving a long letter to be read to the assembled convention in which he expressed his concerns for the future of West Texas ranching. Slaughter believed that the Texas legislature was attempting to break up the large ranches of West Texas. He felt that the stockmen of the region deserved better treatment. He insisted that cattlemen were responsible not only for driving "the savages from our frontier" but also for increasing the value of the land by bringing "civilization" to it. "Nature has designed Western and Northern Texas for a great pasture," he wrote. "It is the finest grazing country in the world and fit for little else."

Slaughter also asked that the new law require cattlemen to take leases "in such bodies as will prevent them from taking the watered and leaving the unwatered lands—say take the lands in a square or as nearly as may be—the bad with the good." The convention agreed with Slaughter and adopted a resolution calling upon the legislature to permit the leasing of school land at two cents per acre for not less than twenty years. On April 12, 1883, the legislature enacted the lease legislation, but it took a more realistic position than that of the cattlemen by providing for ten-year contracts at four cents per acre.

In spite of the four-cent price, ranchers rushed to take advantage of the lease law. Under its provisions, in January 1884 Slaughter leased from the state all the alternate sections contained in his Texas and Pacific lease and additional land in Dawson and Martin counties totaling 340,000 acres. Most cattlemen, including Slaughter, refrained from competing with each other for leases and continued to honor "range rights."

Because ranchers did not compete for the land, the lease act did not create as much revenue for the state as expected. As a result the State

Land Board in February 1885 raised the minimum charge to eight cents. Many of the cattlemen refused to pay and went to court, claiming that the board had no authority to increase the lease price. After a lengthy fight, the state supreme court ruled the action of the board unlawful because it had set a price higher than that stipulated by law.[2]

The introduction of barbed wire complicated the situation. With the new invention, cattlemen enclosed portions of the public domain, and this led to fence cutting. Although he had fenced much of his holdings, Slaughter fortunately enjoyed relative freedom from both the leasing and fence-cutting conflicts, largely because of the isolation of his West Texas ranch, far west of the frontier of the disgruntled farmers and small stockmen.

Meanwhile, Slaughter's five-year lease of 192,000 acres of railroad land expired in 1886. Faced with the possibility of losing his lands to prospective purchasers, Slaughter bought 128,000 acres in the corners of Howard, Martin, Dawson, and Borden counties from the Texas and Pacific for $220,485.82. However, by redeeming the railroad's bonds which he had purchased on a glutted market, he reduced the actual cost by more than half. The acquisition, combined with previous smaller purchases, gave Slaughter title to approximately 140,000 acres, that, added to the leases and nonlease land in use, totaled more than 600,000 acres, an area about the size of an average West Texas county.

Because of opposition, largely from East Texans, to the Land Laws of 1879 and the resulting acquisition of millions of acres in large blocks by corporations, especially foreign, the legislature in 1887 attempted to settle the problems of both the sale and lease of public lands. A new law, passed April 1, 1887, provided that up to four sections could be purchased by "actual settlers" for two dollars per acre for unwatered land and three dollars for watered. Designed to prevent cattlemen from acquiring large holdings, the law required the purchaser to reside on the land for three consecutive years and to prove such residency. Also the Lease Law was revised. Lands classified as grazing could be held for the duration of the lease without fear of sale, but length of rental was reduced to five years at four cents per acre. On April 8, 1889, the legislature again modified the law to allow lands north of the Texas and Pacific Railway, which included the Long S Ranch, to be leased for six years. Under these conditions, Slaughter periodically renewed many of his leases for the next twenty years and was able to maintain his solid block of land despite growing competition.[3]

The tremendous growth of ranching in West Texas soon led to overstocking. By the early 1880s, even the virgin grass of the upper Colorado and Brazos valleys had been depleted. Slaughter and others then sought relief on vast expanses of the Llano Estacado, where adequate water was available only by the use of windmills.

Slaughter may have been the first of the large ranchers in West Texas to use windmills. Other ranches began relying on wells for watering cattle in 1885, but Slaughter probably constructed windmills soon after fencing his land in 1883. By the end of 1885, he had eight wells in Dawson County, ranging in depth from sixty to eighty-four feet. The investment—approximately four hundred to seven hundred dollars per well—proved to be wise, for it enabled him to survive some later droughts.

Meanwhile, with favorable weather conditions, most West Texas ranchers had continued to overstock their ranges. The years 1880 and 1881 had been relatively dry, averaging only sixteen inches rainfall on the South Plains, but 1882 through 1885 were wet. Nearly twenty-five inches were measured at Fort Elliott in Wheeler County in 1882; three years later, thirty-seven inches fell at the same location, seven inches in the month of June. On that basis ranchers expected annual precipitation to be twenty-eight inches or more, not realizing that normal rainfall was approximately eighteen to twenty inches. As a result West Texas cattlemen continued to add cattle to already crowded ranges.[4]

Three years of ideal weather dramatically came to an end in West Texas on January 16, 1885. A Slaughter cowboy herding cattle on the Long S could hardly believe what he saw when the storm struck:

> One evening about three o'clock a great black cloud appeared in the north. We knew a blizzard was coming and that a drift [of the cattle] was certain. In less than an hour the storm was raging, but it was nearly midnight before the lead of the herd began to pass. We were on the very center of the line of the drift and the ground was covered with six or seven inches of snow. . . . All night the blizzard raged and all night the mighty avalanche of cattle moved before it.

Surviving cattle from the Panhandle joined by those of the Long S pushed through drift fences and moved with the driving blizzard as far south as the Pecos and Devil's rivers. The situation was dismal. Thousands piled up against fences and perished; other hundreds drowned in rivers; and still many others died in bog holes or of thirst on the open prairies.[5]

In early February a number of South Plains cattlemen met at Colorado City and laid plans to retrieve the scattered herds. Cooperatively, each of twelve ranches contributed a wagon and ten to fifteen men for the task. Gus O'Keefe, Slaughter's Long S foreman, was chosen to coordinate the roundup. From Big Spring the cow outfits moved south to the Pecos and then turned north to drive the stock back.

Colonel Slaughter was on hand at Big Spring to help tally the cattle as they crossed the Texas and Pacific tracks. There he persuaded the railroad to provide water at one of its large tanks for twenty-five thousand head until owners could claim them. From Big Spring, Slaughter's cattle, about ten thousand head, were driven north to Sulphur Springs, then to the Rattlesnake division. Troughs had to be constructed along the trail to provide water. "Cattle were poor, and not much grass, horses pretty well ridden down, and all those things put together made it mighty bad," wrote Rufe O'Keefe, brother to the Slaughter foreman. The storm took a heavy casualty in Slaughter cattle; many years later, Rufe O'Keefe estimated the loss at five thousand head, but Bob Slaughter, who afterward became manager, set the figure at ten thousand, or 50 percent of the Long S herd. Regardless, the number lost was significant.

The following spring brought some relief. The heavy winter snow provided green grass, the surviving cattle quickly fattened, and prices turned upward, enabling Slaughter to recuperate some of his loss at the marketplace. Meanwhile, he restocked his range with ten carloads of bulls acquired in Denver and dispatched fencing crews to enclose the range permanently. A welcome rain in June brought additional relief.[6]

Unfortunately, the June rain was the last moisture of significance in West Texas for over a year. As the drought persisted, ranchers were forced to market their herds prematurely, a move which, of course, drove prices downward. Although there were a few showers on the South Plains in late summer of 1886, the drought continued into 1887.

Meanwhile, the situation was much worse on the northern Great Plains. There the winter of 1886–1887 was a final disaster for many cattlemen. A deep snow in November and a raging blizzard in late January destroyed the already weakened drought-stricken cattle by the thousands. "When spring finally came," according to historian Ray Allen Billington, "cattlemen saw a sight they spent the rest of their lives trying to forget. Carcass piled upon carcass in every ravine, gaunt skeletons staggering about on frozen feet, heaps of dead bodies along the fences, trees stripped bare of their bark—those were left as monuments to the thoughtless greed of ranchers." The hard winter signaled the end of the open range cattle industry.

Although the South Plains of Texas was spared from severe weather during the winter of 1886–1887, Slaughter and other cattlemen were not as fortunate the following year. A blizzard that struck on January 14, 1888, took a heavy toll. Three hundred head of Slaughter cattle froze to death, piled against new barbed wire fences, and hundreds of others, for the second time in three years, drifted southward to the Pecos River. On January 28 Slaughter sent fresh horses and corn from Dallas to the ranch and then headed west himself once again to supervise the roundup. There he found that most of his herds had been able to drift through fences but were scattered across one hundred miles of West Texas prairies to the south of the Long S. And on his own ranch, he found "cattle by the thousands" that, after breaking down fences, had drifted from ranches even as far north as the Canadian River. Although immense, the death loss on the South Plains was not as high as it had been on the North Plains during the previous winter.[7]

If disastrous weather were not enough of a problem, the situation for ranchers was worsened by national policy changes. On July 23, 1885, President Grover Cleveland ordered the immediate removal from the Cheyenne-Arapaho Reservation of the 210,000 head of cattle placed there by Texas and other cattlemen, including the 8,000 head owned by Hunter, Evans, and Slaughter.

Trouble on the reservation had been brewing almost from the beginning of the lease period. Dissident bands of Indians opposed the cattlemen's presence. On May 4, 1884, Cheyenne Chief Running Buffalo was murdered while trying to extract a toll from Texas drover E. M. Horton; theft from both whites and Indians was prevalent; and in addition to 160 cowboys employed on the reservation by cattlemen, at least 200 whites roamed at will. When convinced that the removal of the cattle would quiet the Indians, Cleveland, on July 23, 1885, ordered the stockmen to remove their herds from the reservation within forty days. For those involved the order was a major setback, for apparently they faced the alternatives of returning their herds to overcrowded and drought-stricken ranges of Texas or going to a depressed market. Hunter, Evans, and Slaughter, however, sought other alternatives and were the first to leave. They sent a part of their eight thousand head to market in late August and drove the remainder to a lease approximately fifty miles north of the Cheyenne-Arapaho pasture and along Medicine Lodge Creek southeast of Kiowa, Kansas. There they held their herd in anticipation of a more favorable market.

By then the price of cattle, which had hit an 1882 high of seven cents a pound, had slipped to three cents. The forced marketing, as a result of the exodus from the Cheyenne-Arapaho Reservation and the drought in Texas, drove the price downward even further. Then following the bitter winter of 1886–1887, the market bottomed in October 1887 at less than one cent a pound, and at the end of 1888, the price had climbed to only two and two-fifths cents.[8]

The disastrous weather and the price collapse ruined many cattlemen, both big and small. Worst affected were the investor-owned land and cattle companies that had rushed into the industry following the 1879–1882 bonanza. Headquartered in the Texas Panhandle, the 600,000-acre Francklyn Land and Cattle Company, although stocked with 75,000 head of cattle, folded in 1886 because it could not meet its land and bond payments. The Kentucky Cattle Raising Company, located in Crosby County and publicized as a "model Texas ranch" in 1885, sustained severe financial losses and collapsed in bankruptcy in 1893. Similarly, the English-owned Espuela Land and Cattle Company (Spur Ranch) never fully recovered from heavy losses sustained during the January 1888 blizzard. The T-Anchor Ranch, in Randall County, began in 1888 to sell its land as a result of its losses.

Among survivors of the severe weather and depression was C. C. Slaughter. Throughout the ordeal he remained optimistic. "I do not regard the outlook as gloomy as many of you seem to believe," he told a reporter in January 1886. "The rise and fall of beef is periodical in its nature. . . . A rise in the market causes everything in the shape of beef to be shipped in . . . and the price gets lower and lower. . . . At about the period when everyone has about made up his mind that there is more money in hogs, sheep, horses, mules, and small grain than anything else, . . . the production of beef is neglected and very naturally the prices go up."[9]

As prices continued to decline in 1886, however, Slaughter saw the collapse in a different light. By October he and other cattlemen were blaming a "Beef Trust." Defined as "a few individuals whose power of purchase and ease in combining to regulate the price of beef cattle everywhere and prevent to a large extent wholesale competition," the "trust," to Slaughter, was the major villain. Slaughter explained to a reporter his opinion of how the trust functioned. The price of beef, he said, was regulated not by demand and supply but by the "sweet will" of the "Big Four," Armour, Swift, Hammond, and Morris. Even though cattle prices were the lowest in many years, consumers were still paying as much for beef as when cattle were selling at seven dollars per hundred:

> Gregory, Cooley, and Company, for instance, may have a consignment of cattle for which they are desiring to get their very best for the consignor. Early in the day Armour sends a man to them who offers a price below that they can sell for. Late in the day, Swift's man goes and offers a still lower price. He is followed by an agent from Nel Morris who offers a still smaller figure. Hamlin's [*sic*] man brings up the rear with a still smaller offer and gets the cattle for next to nothing. In this way they control the beef market of the United States and the cattlemen are powerless against them. The "Big Four" are greater enemies to the cattle business than all the drouth, pleuropneumonia, and Texas fever, for these three come and go, are intermittent, but the "Big Four" go on forever.

On February 9, 1887, Slaughter attended the International Range Association in Denver, where he was elected a director. There he heard Edward M. McGillin, a Cleveland, Ohio, merchant and heavy investor in the western livestock industry, charge that the meat packers were responsible for control of the market and were bankrupting the cattle raiser. McGillin advocated the creation of a huge cattle trust as the best means for coping with the packers' monopoly. Calling for the creation of a hundred-million-dollar corporation, he claimed that such a trust could "arrange, manage, [and] sell every animal from the time it was dropped a calf until it was beef in the consumer's basket."

McGillin's idea struck a harmonious chord with the assembled cattlemen. Within three months the stock raisers had formed the American Cattle Trust, an organization patterned after that of the Standard Oil Trust. Slaughter was named to its board of directors. [10]

Meanwhile, Slaughter personally continued the fight against the meat packing combination. On March 9 he told the Northwest Texas Cattle Raisers Association in Fort Worth that "if there ever was a time in [the] history of the association when the interests of the stockmen demanded thorough organization, it is now, since we stand face to face with a combination east that makes the outlook look gloomy indeed. A closer organization among ourselves and joint organization with other associations is the only hope of safety." Slaughter felt that an all-Texas trust could control "a home market from which Texas could send out to the world dressed meat instead of steers." In conclusion he challenged his fellow cattlemen with the statement that "Providence only helps those who help themselves. . . . What are you going to do?"

Slaughter carried on the fight against the beef trust to the national level. At St. Louis on November 20, 1888, he was named the first president of the National Beef Producers and Butchers Association, organized to present a unified front against the "Big Four" packers. As president of the newly formed association, he circulated newsletters urging the passage of livestock inspection laws and attacking the "Beef Combine." The Chicago packers were undercutting local butchers, he insisted, and cattle raisers should stand by the butcher interests, "not for the purpose of destroying the packing houses, but to keep alive the butcher competition and protect ourselves." [11]

While in St. Louis, Slaughter had opportunity to testify before the United States Senate's Select Committee on the Transportation and Sale of Meat Products. Created by the Senate on May 16, 1888, the committee had traveled throughout the Midwest seeking evidence to support the cattlemen's argument that a combination existed. On November 18, 1888, the committee, headed by George G. Vest of Missouri, heard the testimony of several prominent cattlemen, including Texas stock raisers Dudley Snyder, A. P. Bush, and Slaughter. Slaughter testified that the cattle depression was the direct result of the beef combine. He pointed out that the Chicago-based packers had destroyed an excellent market at St. Louis, where in 1882 he had received the highest price for which he had ever sold cattle. Soon after, he had found the St. Louis market weakened because cattle were simply shipped on to Chicago. Slaughter said that he then shipped cattle to Kansas City, tested the market there, and often went on to Chicago. "As soon as I would go to Chicago, before the cattle arrived, it would be known what I was offered at Kansas City, and it naturally brought me to thinking this is a strange coincidence; these fellows tell me just what I was offered at Kansas City." The price he was offered, Slaughter said, was "just . . . enough more to pay the freight." Then he tried St. Louis and encountered the same results. "If I did not sell in St. Louis, and if I went on the passenger train to Chicago ahead of my cattle, the next morning, before their arrival, I would find that the offer was known that was made for them in St. Louis."

Impressed with the testimony gathered, particularly Slaughter's, the committee reported to the Senate that stockmen could find "no competition among buyers, and if they refused to take the first bid are generally forced to accept a lower one." Denying that overproduction was a major factor in the cattle depression, the committee concluded that the cattlemen's plight was caused by the abnormal and "ruinous centralization of the cattle market" and that it "is impossible that the Chicago market should continue to control the cattle interest of the whole country as it does now." On the other hand, it continued, the overmarketing of cows and calves had driven prices downward, but with the continued growth of population and the decrease in availability of rangeland, the price would eventually improve.

In 1890 in spite of the committee's report, Slaughter was still attacking the packers. In mid-March he and his brothers John and Bill attended the Interstate Convention of Cattlemen at Fort Worth. There they heard a letter read from Texas Governor Lawrence Sullivan Ross which echoed C. C. Slaughter's sentiment that something must be done about the beef trust. Ross stated that something "permanent and radical" was needed to remove the "syndicate" that dominated the cattle market, for "the price of every cow in the land is settled by its decree." Ross lauded "the cordon of fearless cattlemen like the Slaughters, Goodnight, Browning, Reynolds, Mathews, Carter, Harmisons, Braggs, Gholson, Elkins, Lovings, and a Score of others . . . who for years have been the exemplars of the chivalrous generosity and bravery which made them the hero of tales recounted the world over, [but] in many instances they have been dealt with as men who have no claim to protection." [12]

The cattlemen's national organizations did little to halt the decline in cattle values. The American Cattle Trust purchased a packing plant and feed pens and negotiated canning contracts with the French and Belgian governments but did not long survive. Dissension among directors and management, overvaluation of stock certificates, and lack of support from cattlemen doomed it to failure. By the summer of 1890, its trustees were forced to absorb large losses. However, because Slaughter's role in the business affairs of the trust was minimal, his losses apparently were not severe.

Slaughter's efforts as president of the National Producers and Butchers Association also brought little result. After circulating a newsletter condemning the "Beef Trust," the association apparently did little else and may not have met again. It was not until 1921, two years after Slaughter's death, that his work was rewarded when Congress curtailed the monopolistic practices of the big packers by the Packers and Stockyards Act.

There is no evidence that, at the time, Slaughter or the other cattlemen fully understood the complexities behind the depression. Obviously, during the early 1880s, they were responsible for considerable overproduction. This, combined with premature marketing of low-grade cattle, as a result of the drought and the necessity to withdraw from the Cheyenne-Arapaho Reservation, led to rapidly dwindling market prices. Demand simply did not keep pace with supply. Furthermore, the cattlemen failed to recognize the "boom-bust" nature of economy. James A. Cox, writing eight years after the price collapse, best explains what actually happened.

> The magnificent prices . . . in the early eighties were succeeded by prices which, while in some instances . . . left a nominal margin of profit, took away the gold-mine appearance and reputation of trade and made the earning of a livelihood much more common than the amassing of a fortune. . . . Undue haste to become rich and to find the road to wealth led to the killing of the goose to secure the golden egg, which it was apparently willing to lay at respectable intervals.

In spite of droughts, blizzards, the packers' trust, price collapse, and depression, some longtime cattlemen, including C. C. Slaughter, survived. Throughout the ordeal Slaughter saw the depression as temporary. He told a reporter in May 1886 that, in spite of the 20 percent decrease in the price of a steer, "still there is money in him, if a man understands his business." Even when prices for his cattle tumbled to $2.15 per hundred in November 1887, he remained optimistic. "I can raise a good beef steer," he said, "for $20 and make a living," but even so, he anticipated a sharp increase in prices during 1888.[13]

To survive the cattle depression, however, Slaughter had to utilize all his resources, experience, and skill. When pressed by creditors, he would wire his manager, Gus O'Keefe, to gather the necessary number of fat cattle and young heifers and ship them to market, a practice one Slaughter cowboy, at least, could not understand.

> I wondered why a man like Lum [C. C.] Slaughter would ever get in a tight for money. . . . I could never see why they bought a herd of cattle, pay some cash and make notes on the balance. They were buying cattle all the time, that is for several years. I know those notes had to be paid with fat cattle, Steer money, as far as it would go, and then make a run on fat cows and heifers, which they did not want to do, especially on young heifers for they were trying to build up this herd. . . . When Slaughter used to come to the outfit, he and Gus would sit up half the night and talk and plan how they would manage.

To have the fattest cows possible for sale, Slaughter employed a veterinarian in April 1887 to teach his cowboys how to spay cows. (Spayed cows usually gained extra weight.) The spaying operation on two thousand cows was completed in two weeks. The following November, Slaughter shipped four trains of fattened cows from Big Spring to market. Unfortunately, in December his steer herd, gathered at Big Spring for shipment, stampeded and was not shipped.[14]

Slaughter also survived the depression because he was in position to take advantage of an unusual opportunity. In March 1886 he contracted to the newly established XIT Ranch ten thousand head of one- and two-year-old steers and heifers for a reported fourteen dollars a head. The largest fenced ranch in the world, the XIT stretched over three million acres along the western side of the Texas Panhandle. Its immediate need for large numbers of stock cattle and its close proximity to the Long S meant that there would be no expensive freight rates to pay and that Slaughter was provided a good market.

Before delivering any of his own herd to the XIT, Slaughter, acting as a middleman, contacted several cattle suppliers for additional cattle. One company, Webb and Webb Cattle Company of Albany, pleaded with Slaughter for the exclusive opportunity to fill his request. "We know of your standing as one of the leading cattlemen of the state, and if you will give us *half a chance* . . . we can fill your order for you to your entire satisfaction." Webb's prices, however, apparently did not allow the margin of profit Slaughter desired, and by March he had decided to supply the XIT with cattle from his own range.

The Slaughter-XIT deal attracted statewide attention. "The terms of the foregoing trades are among the most carefully guarded secrets of the mysterious cattlemen and it would require the craft of a mind reader to get at them," reported the *Dallas Morning News* on March 27,

1886. "The oldest inhabitant even hasn't the ghost of an idea as to the price received," stated the *Texas Livestock Journal*. Slaughter, however, reportedly received $140,000 cash for the ten thousand cattle.[15]

Slaughter scheduled delivery of the cattle to the XIT in June, July, and September 1886. Winter losses and dry weather during the spring, however, made it difficult to meet the timetable. It was not until summer that the cowboys were able to assemble the cattle. Most of the herd were from the Long S, driven to the Running Water Ranch by way of Tahoka Lake and Yellow House Canyon near present-day Lubbock. Slaughter, the Morrison brothers, and W. D. Johnson met at the Running Water to supervise the stock selection. Johnson's presence soon caused a row. When Slaughter ordered Rufe O'Keefe to deliver the cattle, Johnson wanted to go along to supervise the job but, fearing his presence would delay the final transfer, Slaughter persuaded his partner instead to help him move a small herd to Tule Canyon, northeast of the Running Water Ranch. "That would keep Johnson busy and keep him from going with me and the boys," recalled O'Keefe. "He [Slaughter] did not want to hurt Johnson's feelings."

With the main herd on its way to the XIT, Slaughter, the Morrisons, and Johnson set out for Tule Canyon. "You fellows are getting too old to turn cowboy," O'Keefe chided. Perhaps they were. While on the twenty-five-mile drive, Slaughter and Johnson clashed. "After awhile, Slaughter looked down the creek where Johnson was, and instead of Johnson riding fast and trying to hold the cattle up so they could round them up, he was just poking along letting the cattle pass him and scatter down the creek," reported a Slaughter cowboy who witnessed the scene. Slaughter then took a "slicker" in his hand, got ahead of Johnson's cattle, and "ran into them with that slicker hollering and yelling at the top of his voice . . . and liked to run the cattle over Johnson. I expected that was what he wanted to do. . . . [Slaughter] told him to get back home and stay there and told him he should not have anything to do with the management of that ranch." Slaughter later apologized to Johnson, but their relationship thereafter remained strained.

While delivering the second herd to the XIT, the drovers had to send for Slaughter to come to their aid. The thirsty cattle had stampeded into the dry bed of alkaline Tahoka Lake, about five miles northeast of the present town of Tahoka, and had begun milling about. Unable to control the herd, trail boss O'Keefe quickly sent word of the situation to Slaughter, who was at the German Springs headquarters of the Long S. Gathering all the available cowboys, Slaughter armed them with guns and hastened to Tahoka Lake. Under his command the cowboys rode to the edge of the herd, fired their guns to frighten the cattle, and coaxed from the bed about a hundred at a time. After many hours of desperate work, all the cattle were finally driven from the lake and started north again. Slaughter, however, nearly lost his eyesight; he never recovered entirely from the injury caused by the alkali dust stirred by the milling cattle.

In spite of delivery problems, the XIT deal assured Slaughter's survival of both the drought and depression. By clearing his range of ten thousand head, or one-fourth of his herd, he was in a position to handle the three-year drought. The sale also provided him with needed revenue, and when that proved deficient, his strong banking ties provided him with credit lines. As a result Slaughter was able to wait patiently for the end of the drought and depression. In early September 1888, he sold eighty fat steers for $3.10 per hundred, a price which signaled an upturn in the long depressed market. At the same time, September rains ended the three-year drought. Encouraged by a mild winter and a gradual increase in price, Slaughter, in the spring of 1889, shipped five thousand head of cattle to Kiowa, Kansas, to fatten for marketing.[16]

The end of the depression also coincided with a major change in Slaughter's ranch management. His longtime, capable manager of the Long S, Gus O'Keefe, taking advantage of cheap land and cattle prices, left Slaughter's service in 1888 to run his own ranch. Named to replace him was Slaughter's eighteen-year-old son Robert L. ("Bob") Slaughter.

The first of his boys to assume a management position, the headstrong and sometimes boisterous Bob was well suited to the rugged outdoor ranch life of West Texas. George, the eldest, following the completion of his education, played an active part in the directorship and management of the Running Water Ranch. As soon as they were old enough to ride horses, the three younger brothers, E. Dick, Alexander, and C. C., Jr., worked as cowhands on the ranches during the summers. Unlike Bob, each earned college degrees and became secretaries for their father.

The disagreements with his partner W. D. Johnson made the Slaughter operation a family business. On July 16, 1890, Slaughter dissolved the six-year-old partnership in the Running Water Land and

Cattle Company by trading his half interest in the cattle, horses, and equipment for Johnson's interest in the land, approximately 89,000 acres in patented holdings and a similar amount in leases. George Slaughter was appointed manager, a position he would hold for the next twenty-five years. The ranch was soon restocked with cattle from the Long S. Although the future of the cattle business was still uncertain, Slaughter correctly surmised that the worst had passed. Retrenchment in the face of the financial crisis produced fenced ranges, strong leases, and a completely family-oriented management. And with the elimination by the depression of a number of competitors, prices slowly recovered. The next two decades more than made up for the tribulation of the last half of the 1880s. [17]

5

Royalty on the Range
Ancient Briton and Sir Bredwell

Ranching in West Texas and on the Great Plains has passed through only two major phases during its one-hundred-year history—the open range and controlled stock farming. During the 1890s technical developments, especially barbed wire and the windmill, combined with the steady intrusion of the farmers' frontier, hastened the transition of open range ranching into modern stock farming. Many of the plains ranches did not survive the decade. C. C. Slaughter's cow empire, however, not only survived but became one of the largest producers of fine beef cattle.

For nearly forty years, Slaughter had utilized the open range. Cheap land, free grass, and vast unrestricted prairies had contributed to the building of .is vast West Texas empire. However, by 1890 hundreds of miles of tightly strung barbed wire fences and scores of windmills had brought the cattleman's bonanza to an end. Furthermore, the advancing farmers' frontier heralded a promising agricultural future. In the West Texas–Panhandle region, thirty-four counties were organized from 1888 to 1892. Although he was deeply involved in bank expansion, real estate acquisition in Dallas, industrial investments, and philanthropic activities, Slaughter continued to devote much of his time to his West Texas ranches; such problems as drought and troublesome family management required considerable attention.

Unpredictable weather on the plains was a constant problem. Although a mild winter and adequate rainfall insured a good year for the region in 1890, short dry spells began to plague West Texas early the next year. Rainfall in September forestalled a severe drought, but the dry weather damaged winter feed grasses.

The drought continued into 1892. Although the Long S was not severely affected, the Running Water Ranch received little or no rain throughout the spring. In the summer the drought spread throughout the entire South Plains. By the spring of 1893, West Texas pastures were barren, and cattle were dying by the thousands. The result was dramatic. Calf production on ranches dropped by as much as 40 percent. The neighboring ranch on the south of the Long S, the Magnolia Ranch, which branded 6,000 calves in 1893, ceased operation after branding only 160 head the following year.[1]

The drought was the worst in the history of the Slaughter range. Nearby Colorado City, where the average rainfall was twenty-two inches annually, had only eight and a half inches in 1893. In 1894 no rain fell until May.

The dry weather soon forced Slaughter to seek grass elsewhere. In April 1893 he sent five thousand head by rail to Glasgow, Montana, and contracted with a Council Grove, Kansas, feeder, Frank Lower, to place several hundred head in feedlots. Other cattle were driven to leased pastures in New Mexico and the Panhandle where the drought was not as severe. By 1895 Slaughter had ten thousand head on leased ranges in Montana and Wyoming. Such movements helped minimize his losses.

Following a June 1894 tour of the Long S, Colonel Slaughter reported a dismal but not hopeless situation to his son George. "The grass in the Rattlesnake [pasture] and especially in German [Springs] seems too gone. Thousands of acres show no sign of either grass or weeds. The grass in the ballance [*sic*] of the range looks as though it will be good." For the spring of 1894, the Colonel estimated his losses at 3 percent, or one thousand head, due primarily to lack of water.

In spite of the drought, Slaughter marketed a large number of cattle. In the fall of 1894, he sold $100,000 worth, including 210 head which averaged 1,212 pounds each. Although the Long S Ranch lost money, perhaps for the first time in its history, sales from cattle fed in Kansas, from the Running Water, and from leased pastures in Montana offset the damage caused by the drought.

The dry weather ended on the Slaughter range in dramatic fashion. In May 1894 a vicious thunderstorm raked the Long S Ranch, destroying the headquarters at German Springs. The storm "blowed the old office all to pieces . . . ," reported Slaughter to his son George. "Twisted all the trees off at the ground, broke the corral down, took off the windmill I don't know where." By the time the drought-breaking rains came, most of West Texas had been cleared of cattle (and prospective homesteaders as well). Grass on the unstocked ranges grew back rapidly; by October 1894, ranchers were indicating that both cattle and winter pastures were in excellent shape.[2]

In addition to coping with a severe drought, Slaughter simultaneously had to deal with a number of family problems. By 1893 his twenty-three-year-old son Bob, who had managed the Long S for five years, was married and seemingly settled into the comfortable life of a West Texas ranch manager. Likewise, his thirty-one-year-old son George, manager of the Running Water Ranch, married on February 1, 1893, the daughter of a prominent Plainview merchant, J. N. Donohoo, and settled in a comfortable home on his ranch. However, for reasons never explained, the two brothers had developed drinking habits not acceptable to their father. Vowing to reform, they and younger brother Dick went to Kansas City in January 1894 to take the "Kealy cure" for overindulgence in alcoholic drinks. Colonel Slaughter admonished them to get a thorough treatment and at the same time revealed his own obsession for frugality.

> Whatever is worth doing should be done well. As you have all undertaken this cure as it is called, to the whole hogg [sic] or none. Of course you ought to have been men enough to let it alone without this. . . . Keep a memorandum of every cent you spend and don't spend anything you can do without.

A day later Slaughter learned that Bob had taken his wife on the trip. Angrily, he wrote George (with whom he could communicate best) that he could not tolerate expense-paid vacations.

> You are well aware that I am very easy with my children. Again you know I am very *determined* when I get roused up and I tell you now I am determined to run my business in the best business principles I can and to master it too. . . . I never dreamed I would have to furnish the money to take familys [sic] on a trip. A hint to the wise is sufficient.

Whatever the purpose of the trip, the Slaughter brothers were back on the job by the end of February, apparently cured either by the treatment or by their father's reprimand, since there is no further mention of the alcohol problem in Slaughter's correspondence with his sons.

Pressured financially by the national depression which followed the Panic of 1893, Slaughter continued to monitor expenses carefully. Wages for cowhands were kept to a minimum. Son Bob earned only seventy-five dollars a month as manager of the vast Long S. George wanted a loan of five thousand dollars to establish a bank in Plainview, but his reluctant father tactfully replied that, due to loss of money loaned to C. C.'s brothers, John and Bill, his son should look elsewhere. "I can't loan you the five thousand without borrowing." As an alternative he suggested that George create a banking company and invite his father-in-law and a few other merchants to invest two or three thousand dollars each. "Be a director and attend to your own affairs, etc.," Slaughter encouraged his son, coyly adding that he could "arrange" for a two-thousand-dollar loan.

In January 1895 Colonel Slaughter separated the personal and ranch banking accounts of his sons and ordered George and Bob to submit monthly statements of expenditures for payroll and provisions and quarterly summary statements. "I think by doing this I can keep expenses straight without so much work," he explained to George, "and this is the best business way I can think of giving in detail what is bought and what for, also what is sold and what for. I wish to get our matters arranged on as easy a basis as possible."

By early 1895 conditions had improved significantly for Slaughter. Owning title to more than 250,000 acres of land, with 37,000 head of cattle on his ranches and with his own bank in Dallas, he admitted, conditionally, that he was doing well. In a letter to George concerning the Plainview banking venture, he modestly related, "From all appearances we are all ok financially, and as this is the first year for a long time I felt this way, don't you think we had better lay on our oars this year and let developments show us which way the financial tide is drifting us[?]"

Slaughter ignored his own advice. In 1895 he increased shipments of cattle to Montana and Wyoming ranges, stocking those pastures with three- and four-year-old steers. Angered at rising costs of rail shipments and losses of cattle in transit, Slaughter in 1896 threatened to trail drive his northern-bound cattle. Perhaps due to that and to the loss of 120 head during the April 1896 shipment, he was able to obtain from the railroads a guaranteed rate of $2.00 per head for shipments to northern pastures, a reduction from a high of $5.90 in 1885. Because of the rate reduction, Slaughter expanded his cattle-feeding operations in Kansas and other midwestern points. In February 1896 he proposed to furnish Kansas feeder Frank Lower cattle at $27.00 per head to feed and pasture for six months prior to sale with each to share equally the profit or loss. He explained to George the advantage of such an arrangement.

> We cannot get our cattle down here [to Dallas] to the cotton seed meal [because of the threat of tick fever] and if we have them fed which I think we will have to do in the future we must look to Kansas, Nebraska and Montana. . . . By this we will obtain the feed cheaper than we could any other way. . . . If those men make any money we will get 1/2 of it and a fair price for our cattle.[3]

Through similar arrangements, Slaughter supplied Kansas and Nebraska feeders for a number of years.

Ironically, Slaughter was able to use the national depression of 1893 and the drought of 1893–1894 as a means of expanding his own holdings. As a creditor he sometimes obtained pasture leases at low rates through partnership deals or made foreclosures and bargain purchases on leases, cattle, and land. His bank in Dallas, specializing in West Texas cattle business, made loans for land or cattle purchases at 10 percent interest. If Slaughter cosigned the note, he personally held the lease, cattle, or land as collateral. In at least one instance, he increased his holdings through foreclosure. In 1897 he acquired the lease of the 140,000-acre Tahoka Lake Ranch in Lynn County through foreclosure on a note given by A. J. Harris. Although the ranch contained little patented land, the transaction gave Slaughter a badly needed, well-watered pasture. That year, for an undisclosed amount, he also bought the 64,000-acre TJF Ranch in northeastern Dawson County after its owner, Jesse Evans, went broke. This acquisition, which bordered the Indian Springs division of the Long S, gave Slaughter control of almost the eastern half of Dawson County and increased his patented holdings to nearly 300,000 acres.

The depression and the drought of the 1890s forced West Texas cattlemen to change from raising native longhorns to producing purebred breeding stock. The transition was gradual but far-reaching. Like other stockmen in West Texas, for many years Slaughter had primarily crossbred Durham shorthorns with native stock. In 1880, however, he began limited use of other blooded cattle, particularly Herefords. Hereford cattle, less suited to rigorous trail drives, became popular after railroads extended into the West. Charles Goodnight, however, began building his Hereford herd on the JA in 1883, six years before the Fort Worth and Denver laid its rails in the vicinity of his range, paying $250 per head for twenty registered Hereford bulls. This purchase founded the JA's famous JJ herd.[4]

The next year Slaughter followed Goodnight's example. He purchased ten carloads of Hereford bulls for the Long S and turned them onto the open range with crossbred shorthorn-longhorn cattle. Unlike Goodnight, however, he was not ready to risk purebred stock. Instead, he purposely continued to crossbreed to prevent regression in size and quality. In October 1894 he sent George to Missouri and Illinois to buy shorthorn bulls to breed to his existing admixture of longhorn-shorthorn-Hereford cows. "After a few years, we will probably go back to Herefords," George explained to a reporter as he left for his trip. "I believe in breeding up, without giving cattle any chance to go backward." With the extension of railroads into the plains and the disappearance of cattle trailing, the range cattle industry was poised to adopt a new breed.

The Hereford emerged as the cowmen's favorite. As early as the mid-1880s, it had begun to supplant the shorthorn in midwestern fat stock shows, and in 1886 Herefords won key shows in Kentucky, the heartland for shorthorn breeders. Thereafter, shorthorn and Hereford breeders competed fiercely at stock shows until the Panic of 1893 slowed purchases of expensive purebred stock. As cattle prices began to recover in the mid-1890s, the demand for purebred stock correspondingly increased. By the end of 1896, with cattle prices at 1885 levels and with the enclosure of rangelands (which allowed the use of controlled breeding), purebred stock for the American West became practical and more profitable. The spring of 1897 marked a major turning point in this aspect of the western cattle industry.[5]

C. C. Slaughter was at the forefront of the change. Eager to become a "gentleman breeder," he took the first opportunity to add purebred Hereford cows to his herd. In January 1897 he learned from a longtime friend and debtor, Fount G. Oxsheer, that a prized herd of Hereford cows was for sale. A longtime West Texas cattleman, Oxsheer, while visiting his Diamond Ranch in Hockley County the previous year, had closely examined a herd of nineteen hundred Herefords previously owned by Charles Goodnight. This herd was well known in the Texas cattle industry. Begun by Goodnight in 1874 in Pueblo, Colorado, the cattle had been improved and bred to imported Hereford bulls since 1883. When Goodnight established the JA Ranch in 1876 in partnership with John Adair, the herd was branded JJ. Following Adair's death, Goodnight and Mrs. Adair divided the herd in 1888, Goodnight's portion becoming the ⟩⟩ (Cross-J) cattle. Goodnight later claimed that he "topped" his herd after the division, keeping only the best. He told Slaughter that the remnant was "much better than the JJ herd owned by Mrs. Adair." "This herd of cattle," Goodnight boasted, "taking them for vitality, for form, color and beef making . . . are the best herd of cattle now in the round world."

In 1895 Goodnight sold the Cross-J herd to Midland rancher John Scharbauer, who placed them on his Hockley County pasture adjacent to that of Oxsheer's. Soon after his acquisition, for reasons unknown, Scharbauer decided to sell the herd. Oxsheer negotiated for the cattle but could not meet Scharbauer's price. In January 1897, while doing business with Slaughter at his Dallas bank, Oxsheer mentioned that Scharbauer wanted to sell the herd. Relying entirely on Oxsheer's statement about its quality, Slaughter purchased the cattle sight unseen for fifty thousand dollars.

With undisguised glee he reported his find to George.

> Well, I presume you will think when you read further on in this that I have *done it now*. I have bot [*sic*] $50,000 dollars [*sic*] worth of female cattle and 60 registered bulls. I think this is the best trade I ever made. There is not a drop of Texas blood in those cattle and I don't think there is any such a herd with 1/2 the number in the U.S. Now this throws us to front and there is enough she cattle in them to stock the plains in 20 years.

Planning to receive the herd in May, Slaughter faced an immediate problem. Should the Herefords be placed on the Long S with Durham-longhorns? Would the Running Water Ranch accommodate them and at the same time provide adequate shelter? Oxsheer offered a solution that Slaughter accepted. Oxsheer agreed to pasture the herd on his Hockley County ranch for three to four years at one dollar per head per year and, as a commission, would receive a quarter of the herd.

Slaughter then hastened to improve his herd even more. In company with pioneer Hereford breeder W. S. Ikard (who introduced

Herefords to West Texas in 1876), Kansas stockman O. H. Nelson (whose cattle had formed the nucleus of the improved JJ herd), and son Bob, he visited Hereford farms in Missouri, Iowa, and Illinois in search of new bulls to service his prized herd. From Chicago on April 3, he reported to George that he had purchased fifty-seven head of "the best bulls in America if not the world," including Ancient Briton, "the world's champion Hereford bull."[6]

For Ancient Briton, first-place winner at the 1893 Chicago World's Fair and Columbian Exposition, Slaughter paid $2,500, a new record price for a bull. Imported from England specifically to be shown at the international cattle show, the animal was acclaimed as "the best bull that has gone out of the country [Great Britain] for a good many years," and at the close of the exposition, the *Breeder's Gazette* reported that "American breeders are fully prepared to concede that [owner] Mr. Clough has in Ancient Briton the best bull of the breed now on this side of the pond." Then in May 1897, Slaughter purchased from breeder T. F. B. Sotham additional expensive bulls. One animal, Protection, had won first-place ribbons at state fairs in Wisconsin, Minnesota, and Illinois and at the St. Louis fair in 1896. Slaughter considered Protection to be "a beautiful type of the Hereford breed and [as] near perfection as one could wish." The *Texas Stockman and Farmer* reported that, after the purchase of Protection and three other bulls, Slaughter had "in the estimate of many cattlemen topped what is undoubtedly the best collection of bulls ever owned by one man." Slaughter agreed. With the addition of the prized bulls, he estimated that the total worth of the former Goodnight herd was at least a half million dollars.

Slaughter's rapid purchases amazed livestock breeders. Previous use of thousand-dollar bulls had been limited to the Midwest and Kentucky. Slaughter's dramatic introduction of award-winning Herefords to the plains of West Texas marked an important change not only for his operation but also one for the entire Texas cattle industry. Furthermore, it signaled a major victory for the Hereford breeders over the shorthorn.

In May Slaughter visited the South Plains to see his new acquisitions. While he was there, the whitefaced cattle were received from Scharbauer and turned into Oxsheer's Diamond Ranch. Slaughter then persuaded Oxsheer to rename it the Ancient Briton Hereford Ranch and to subdivide the range into six pastures so that each class of bulls could be bred to a corresponding grade of cows. An unimposing lean-to located six miles west of present-day Levelland served as headquarters.

Slaughter's purebred herd provided him considerable publicity as a breeder of fine cattle. Pictures of his bulls were published in leading stock journals, and the *Texas Stockman and Farmer* printed a full front page engraving of the famous Protection. Slaughter even redesigned his stationery to include a color etching of Ancient Briton and to claim Slaughter as owner of the "Champion Hereford Herd of the World." "I want Ancient Briton indelibly associated with the name C. C. Slaughter," he explained to George. "We are on top, if we can just stay there."[7]

But Slaughter's claim to supremacy did not go unchallenged. In April 1897 the JA Ranch, through its manager Richard Walsh, wrote Slaughter.

> I was very much surprised to see a statement of yours published in the Kansas City Drovers Telegram to the effect that your herd of F cows [Cross-J] were selected from the Paloduro [JA] herd. I have also been told by my friends at Fort Worth that you state there is no comparison between the Adair [JA] herd & yours as yours were topped out of the Adair Herd. These statements are not correct.

Walsh explained that at the time the JJ herd was divided there was no difference in the two. Then he bluntly asked Slaughter not to circulate such reports any further and to contradict such statements whenever possible. After this communication to Slaughter, Walsh informed Mrs. Adair that "there is going to be great rivalry in the Hereford business as Col. C. C. Slaughter of Dallas an old time cow thief now a rich banker has bought the Goodnight share of the JJ herd which if you remember Goodnight sold them two years ago & now Slaughter has bought them & is advertising them every way he can."

Undaunted by Walsh's letter, Slaughter continued to boost his herd and to seek the best Hereford bulls available. When he learned that Sir Bredwell, the champion Hereford bull of the 1898 Omaha Exposition, was for sale, he determined to buy him. "I am fully persuaded in my mind that we ought to own this bull," he confided to George, "although we have some of the same stock, from the fact that we have so many champion bulls on our ranch." Although somewhat concerned about the bull's four-year age, Slaughter felt that no price would be too high and that the new bull would not only enhance the value of his herd through new production but also create new favorable publicity. "We can . . . show the world we mean what we say . . . that we are determined to raise the best Hereford herd in America," Slaughter declared. The only place for a champion bull, he said, was with the champion herd.

> These facts will go down the anals [sic] of history,—Where is the Champion Bull of the world, Ancient Briton? Where is the Champion Bull of America in 1898? Sir Bredwell? On the Plains of Texas. Who owns them? C. C. Slaughter. To my mind, we had better pay ten times the value of this bull alone, than to let him go to another herd.[8]

On March 1, 1899, T. F. B. Sotham's annual Hereford sale at Kansas City attracted widespread attention and a thousand cattlemen. Included were Slaughter; Kirk B. Armour, meat packer and president of the American Hereford Breeders Association; and several other wealthy breeders. Sensing that history was to be made, observers packed into the auction arena and, reported a Kansas City newspaper, when Sir Bredwell was led into the ring, "men took their hats off in deference to as fine a specimen of bull as one might see in a lifetime."

Slaughter opened the bidding at $1,000. Armour and others quickly followed; each bid ranged from $100 to $500 higher. When the bidding reached $2,000, the crowd cheered; when it topped $3,000, the sale ring erupted. Never had there been such a bid. "The $3,000 mark was the signal for throwing hats in the air, jumping up and more cheers," reported the *Drover's Telegram*, "and as each additional bid was made, no matter how small, the crowd became more frantic."

When bidding reached $4,000, several breeders were asked to testify to Bredwell's quality. One man who had visited England stated that Sir Bredwell was a finer specimen than any of the bulls in Herefordshire. Colonel Slaughter then announced that the person who wanted Sir Bredwell more than he did would have to pay dearly.

The bidding then resumed. Armour dropped out, leaving only Slaughter and a Mr. Keyt, representing Hereford breeder Frank Nave of Attica, Indiana. Keyt bid $4,100, Slaughter, $4,500. A reporter carefully described the scene when Slaughter bid $5,000, the highest ever bid for a bull at public auction. At this point Edmondson, the sale master, announced that he would give every person an opportunity to decide whether he wanted to bid above $5,000. Keyt said he was through, and the auctioneer sold the bull to Slaughter. At this point the spectators resembled the operators in a board of trade pit when the market had "gone crazy. The tears were streaming down Mr. Sotham's face as Col. Slaughter and Mr. Kyte [*sic*] were compelled to embrace each other in the sale ring amid the shouts and hat throwing of the throng which packed the room. It was a sight never to be forgotten by those who witnessed it." A spectator at the auction attempted to capture the spirit of the drama in mock Shakespearean verse.

> Slaughter cries . . .
> "Come on my braves; to horse! to horse!
> We'll see who bears the stoutest purse!
> For, know, Sir Bredwell said to me,
> 'I crave your hospitality;'
> Nor will I pause until he reigns
> The Monarch of the Texas plains.
> Lay on, Macbeth! Lay on, McDuff!
> Damned be the first who cries 'enough!'"
> But warily his thrust they meet,
> For valor oft must be discreet.
> At "forty-nine" at last they pause,
> While Slaughter jeers their hopeless cause,
> And boldly shouts, "A hundred more!"
> None answer, and the fight is o'er.
> With cheers the very welkin rings,
> As to his prize the victor springs,
> And, supple as a bounding boy,
> Leaps on his back and weeps for joy.
> No bull fight this side of ancient Spain,
> No gaping wounds, nor heroes slain;
> This verse is but the halting tale
> Of Sotham's annual Hereford sale.

After the shouting subsided, Slaughter explained the reason for his expensive purchase. He was pursuing the policy of pioneer Illinois breeder John D. Gillett, who used thoroughbred bulls on grade cows, and Slaughter added that he defied "the world to produce a better specimen of beef than his." A few days later, he reportedly was offered $7,500 for Sir Bredwell but refused with a curt "not for $10,000."

Slaughter used every opportunity to garner publicity for Sir Bredwell. To transport the famous bull to Texas, he rented a box car with a sign proclaiming, "I am Sir Bredwell and I Am Heading for Colonel

C. C. Slaughter's Ranch in Texas." One newspaper speculated that Slaughter was building a mansion in Texas to house Sir Bredwell and his other valuable bulls. A former cowboy, after watching the famous bull pass through Amarillo on the way to the ranch, expressed in a long poem his resentment that Sir Bredwell would receive better treatment than the cowboys who had herded longhorns:

> But here's to you Sir Bredwell,
> The finest of your kind,
> For they tell me that your equal
> They nowhere now can find.
>
> And they tell me Col. Slaughter
> Has for you a palace built,
> I used to sleep right near your house
> With neither bed or quilt.
>
> I've bivouacked herds upon the spot,
> And the Indian bushwhacked me,
> And now you have a kingdom there—
> The change is great, you see.[9]

Slaughter soon learned that expensive bulls required far more care than range bulls. He was forced to rent special pastures where proper feed and shelter were readily available. Rollie Burns, a Lubbock County stock raiser, boarded several Slaughter bulls for $250 per month. Unaccustomed to paying rent, the Colonel soon sought other arrangements. In 1900 he purchased a two-thousand-acre alfalfa farm in the Pecos valley two miles east of Roswell, New Mexico. The new acquisition, in addition to giving Slaughter a well-protected breeding farm, lent prestige to his entire operation. Appropriately named the "Slaughter Hereford Home," the farm was managed by George Slaughter, who that same year moved from Plainview to Roswell. At the new site, he placed Ancient Briton, Sir Bredwell, and a number of other selected bulls and cows. As with all his projects, Slaughter intended the farm to be the best. "You must exercise your best judgment and when you feel anything should be done, go at it," he instructed a pessimistic George, who was concerned about the cost involved. "We want a model farm and it costs money to get it."

Once the Slaughter Hereford Home was operational, it produced not only purebred calves but badly needed hay for winter feeding. The farm also wintered horses from the Texas ranches and produced fruit and vegetables to supply ranch line camps. As a paying venture, however, the farm fell short of expectations, and in 1906 the Colonel gave serious consideration to selling it. Annual operating expenses often were as great as those on both the large West Texas ranches.

The deaths of Ancient Briton and Sir Bredwell in 1902 and 1904, respectively, did not go unnoticed. Colonel Slaughter, while mourning the death of Ancient Briton, found some consolation because "he has served us well." When Sir Bredwell died two years later, George proposed to have the bull's head dressed and stuffed for hanging in his father's Dallas office and to erect a marble monument in Roswell in its commemoration, but there is no evidence that either project was carried out.[10]

For several years Slaughter reaped a great deal of publicity and premium prices from his sales of improved cattle. Although he had little interest in developing stock for the livestock show circuit, he was elated with the publicity received each time his cattle went to market, especially when they topped those from other Texas ranches. "Our steers sold for ten cents per 100 more than JA's, weight 100# more than the JA, killed 1% better than JA," he gleefully reported to George in late 1900. Perhaps the experiment peaked in 1902, when the first increase from his purebred cattle was sold. In June, when he shipped 5,200 two-year-old steers (including shorthorns, shorthorn-Hereford crosses, and purebred Herefords) from Texas to Montana, the Chicago *Livestock World* quoted Texas cattleman A. B. ("Sugg") Robertson's comment on their superior quality: "It was the greatest herd of steers of one age ever brought together." From Kansas City in September 1902, Slaughter reported to George that his sales of two-year-olds of this herd "topped the market for the year," bringing $8.75 per hundred. "The 2-year-old cattle," he continued, "were pronounced by all who saw them as the best finished load of cattle that has been here this year. . . . I have been selling cattle here for more than 21 years and they were the best cattle I have ever sold, and brought the highest price."

Slaughter's purchases of Hereford cows and famous bulls indeed served him well. In five years he rose to the top in the purebred Hereford business, an accomplishment that brought him strong satisfaction. At the outset of the venture, in April 1897, he confided to George that his actions were based on simple rationale. "I have said to you for the last two years there is a place for the cowman where there is no speculation and that is simply the breeding herd." A month later he penned, "Now is the time to understand [that] what we are working for is the future." He never admitted that he may have been swayed by the glamour associated with large livestock sales. He did indicate, however, that he expected that his purchases would insure a notable place for him and his family in the cattle industry. "I am making a determined effort in my old days to put up the largest and best breed-ing Hereford herd in the world," he explained in confidence. "If [we] don't aim high, we cannot expect to get high."

The Colonel also saw his investment as a means of establishing his sons as quality cattle raisers. "Now at much cost of both labor and thought as well as expense," he indicated to George, "I have tried very hard to put you boys to the front in the cattle business. Hope you will succeed in holding the fort. At the same time you will have many jeal-ous men to try to knock you down and so you must be carefull [*sic*] of both what you say and how you act." [11]

During the following decade, "holding the fort" was to be a major challenge for Slaughter and his sons, but the Colonel's enterprise dur-ing the 1890s proved he was capable of facing new problems. His use of cattle feeding during droughts, his adoption of improved breeding herds, his purchase of prized bulls, and his public promotion of his herds enhanced his reputation as a cattle entrepreneur. However, the focal point of his next challenge would be centered not on cattle but on land, as he would enlarge his empire even more in the face of an ad-vancing farmers' frontier.

6

The "Indivisible" Empire The Lazy S Ranch

An important commodity for western American entrepreneurs has been the availability of free or cheap land. From the beginning of the cattlemen's occupation of West Texas, there had always been ample prairie for use by any stockman willing to risk investment. During the first twenty years of C. C. Slaughter's ranching operations in West Texas, regardless of whether state, railroads, or individuals owned the land, grass generally was available to all stock raisers during favorable seasons. In the 1890s, however, the situation changed dramatically. As cattle prices slowly recovered from the market collapse of 1886–1887, open range cattlemen found their control of land suddenly challenged. Prospective farmers and late-arriving ranchers joined in the competition for the remaining stretches of unplowed grassland. As a result C. C. Slaughter, after having weathered severe droughts, blizzards, and depressions, encountered an even greater challenge— control of the land he had been using for twenty years.

From his first occupation of West Texas prairies, Slaughter had had little difficulty in maintaining inexpensive land leases (see chapter 4). For as little as four cents an acre, he had been able to renew his leases every five or six years. And according to the liberal laws established by the Texas legislature, leased land, if improvements had been made in amounts of one hundred dollars or more, could not be sold by the state until expiration of the lease. Since a cattleman could renew his lease before its expiration, the system promised perpetuation.

With the increased demand for land during the 1890s, however, Slaughter's control over vast portions of West Texas was attacked. The first challenge came in 1893 from the Texas and Pacific Railway. Claiming title to a portion of his 1886 purchase, the railroad sued Slaughter for title to 84,000 acres of the Long S and in December won the case. Slaughter, however, salvaged the loss by leasing the disputed land for two and a half cents an acre.

Slaughter's second challenge came from the state legislature. Once sympathetic toward cattlemen, the lawmakers had shifted gradually to a farmer-oriented position and by the mid-1890s began revising certain laws favorable to stock raisers. The legislature on April 4, 1895, created the Four-Section Act, which struck a devastating blow at Slaughter and other big Texas ranchers. This law provided that a prospective settler could acquire one section of agricultural land and three of grazing land for as little as eighty dollars down with four years to pay. Lands were to be sold only to actual settlers, who were required to reside on the land for three years and to make certain minimum improvements before title could be secured. A subsequent amendment lowered the price of agricultural land to one and a half dollars an acre, thereby reducing the required down payment. With passage of the law, demand for land increased precipitously. Because farmers could use windmills to obtain water in previously unwatered places and construct fences to protect crops, cattlemen could no longer maintain control over large blocks of prairie.

At the same time, West Texas ranchers were faced with a pressing need to enclose the land they used. The importation of purebred cattle required controlled breeding, for no rancher who had invested heavily in fine Hereford cattle wanted a rangy longhorn bull impregnating his herd. Consequently, C. C. Slaughter suddenly found that West Texas no longer had any readily available land. "There is a general raid down at the Ranch on leasing land," he sadly reported to son George in September 1897, "and I expect our free grass is gone and it is going to cost us 7 to 10,000.00 more per year than it has for several years." Yet he knew that if he continued to upgrade his herds he would need additional land. "In this great excitement over the Cattle Business," he wrote, "we will have to meet the plungers in both land and cattle and I wish to secure grass and own it if possible."

To increase his holdings, in 1897 Slaughter purchased, as previously noted, the Tahoka Lake Ranch in Lynn County which contained 1,600 acres of patented land and 140,000 acres of leased land. This acquisition not only offset his loss of Long S lands but gave him a layover point for herd movement between the Long S and the Running Water ranches. During the same year, he also acquired the TJF Ranch in northeastern Dawson County for development into a new home for his purebred Hereford herd. However, because he could not secure title to alternate sections, he continued to look elsewhere for land in solid blocks, unencroachable by persistent nesters. Furthermore, he wanted to locate an additional ranch which he could leave to his children. The Long S, he thought, would become Bob Slaughter's legacy, the Running Water, George's, but there were seven other children. To provide for them, he determined to create a permanent inheritance, "undivided and indivisible."

Slaughter found it difficult to locate any large blocks of land. Most Texas land was surveyed in sections. Alternate sections were deeded to surveyors or railroads, and the remainder were reserved for actual settlers. However, there was still one area on the South Plains in 1897 which offered possibilities. Lying in the heart of the Llano Estacado and passed over by railroads and land speculators, the waterless and arid grasslands in Cochran and Hockley counties had quietly passed from the public domain. In 1883 the state legislature had deeded these lands in blocks of four square leagues (17,712 acres) or less to approximately thirty counties for county local school revenue. Most of the counties which received land were forced to locate their surveys in the unwanted remnant of the public domain. On the South Plains, these surveys were located primarily in Cochran, Hockley, and Bailey counties. Surveyed in Spanish measurements, these tracts wre divided into square leagues and subsequently subdivided into *labores*.

These tracts were still available to prospective ranchers who could persuade the counties to lease or sell. With no surface water available except for a few shallow lakes and buffalo wallows, the arid, often sandy country supported few cattle. Nevertheless, a few ranchers had operated in the area since the early 1880s. The first ranch, the Surratt, was established during the 1880s in southern Cochran County, but most of the region was used by small operators who leased pasturage or simply used the grass free of charge. Unable or unwilling to invest in windmills, none of these cattlemen established a foothold in the area.[1]

After the passage of the Four-Section Act in 1895, which opened the public school land for settlement, the 17,712-acre tracts of nonpublic land in Cochran and Hockley counties became more attractive to displaced cattlemen. During the spring of 1897, R. S. Ferrel obtained leases to 43,000 acres in northeastern Cochran County near present-day Morton, apparently intending to stock it, but in May he sold his lease to M. B. Huling of Reeves County. Huling, who had ranched in the Guadalupe Mountain area of West Texas, was familiar with the arid climate of the western South Plains. After obtaining additional land through purchase, Huling leased his entire tract—93,000 acres—to Fount G. Oxsheer.

Perhaps no man better understood the problems of ranching on the South Plains than did Fount Oxsheer. As early as 1888, he had been grazing cattle in the area, and by May 1897, when Slaughter acquired his Hereford herd, he had several thousand head on his Diamond Ranch in western Hockley County. At that time Oxsheer apparently advised Slaughter of the possibility of acquiring title to a large tract of the western South Plains. He pointed out that very little of the land was individually owned, that much of it could be bought from the counties that owned the four-league blocks, and that the purchase would have to be made through agents since the farmer-dominated commissioners courts would never knowingly sell an acre to a landed cattleman.

Realizing that it was probably the last opportunity to acquire a contiguous large-acreage tract and not wanting to rent pasture for his expensive Hereford bulls, Slaughter decided to acquire a large block of some of the Cochran-Hockley land and contracted with Oxsheer to buy fifty to sixty square leagues, or about 250,000 acres.

Naturally, Slaughter wrote George about his plans for the new venture. "I am of the opinion that it is one of the best ranches in the state that can be obtained in a solid body. . . . If I succeed in getting this ranch, and live long enough to improve it right, I desire to make it an insurance policy for my children, *undivided* and *indivisible* [my italics], until the death of the last one of my family. I think it is the best policy I could leave my children as it will be yielding a profit all the time." The sixty-one-year-old Slaughter knew that he would have to move swiftly if he expected to convert the region into a profitable ranch. Yet he hoped to make it a model ranch that would be the crowning achievement of his life. "It will be one of, if not the greatest legacy, ever left to a family in the nation," he promised his son. "It will be the greatest blood preserve on earth. I am trying to leave a sterling character to go with it, as I think a good name is the most priceless heritage a man can leave."

For Slaughter, the purchase of the new ranch involved at least two problems. First, in 1898 farmers were steadily advancing by the hundreds onto the eastern South Plains. Their intrusion forced land prices upward in areas that had been penetrated by railroads. Second, since the Slaughter name was already associated with large landholdings, farmers (and some cattlemen) opposed his efforts to acquire additional acreage. Anticipating such opposition, Slaughter warned George to keep quiet about the Oxsheer deal. "A word to others would ruin us," he wrote. He instructed Oxsheer to proceed cautiously.[2]

Oxsheer enlisted the aid of A. J. Harris, R. S. Ferrel, John Scharbauer, and W. E. Kaye, all of whom, like himself, were indebted to Slaughter's Dallas bank. Harris, who had sold Slaughter the Tahoka Lake Ranch the previous year and had been leasing sixteen square leagues in Hockley County, quickly proved to be the most successful negotiator. Visiting the Panhandle counties of Armstrong and Randall in March 1898, he obtained title to their four-league blocks. In April he persuaded Ferrel to sell the Carson County tract previously acquired for his own use, and soon afterward he obtained title to Mills and Potter counties' school lands. By the end of July 1898, Harris had presented Colonel Slaughter with deeds to 88,560 acres in Cochran County. Located in a ten-by-fourteen-mile block along Sulphur Draw, the land was then being used by John Beal's St. Louis Cattle Company.

Through Oxsheer, Slaughter obtained the 93,000-acre Huling Ranch from M. B. Huling for $25,000. Since Huling only owned four square leagues of the land, Oxsheer dispatched Ferrel to secure titles to their tracts from the commissioners of Brewster and Coke counties. Ferrel easily obtained title, but as soon as he resold the lands to Slaughter, the commissioners of both counties rejected Ferrel's contract on the basis that they had been deceived. After two years of litigation, Slaughter lost title to the Coke County land but eventually succeeded in winning a similar fight with Brewster County.

John Scharbauer, from whom Slaughter had bought the Goodnight Hereford herd, also helped Oxsheer fulfill his contract by conveying his Martin County tract to Slaughter in 1899 and his Midland County block in April 1900, but due to a title dispute, the transfer of the latter was never executed. Slaughter obtained a third major block directly from Oxsheer. In June 1900 Oxsheer deeded to Slaughter his "west pasture" of the Diamond Ranch, 37,000 acres, the tract that had been the pasture for Slaughter's Hereford herd.[3]

A fourth block for the new ranch was created from parcels of southwestern Hockley County land acquired after several years of bitter disputes and litigation. By 1900 Slaughter's agents had obtained title to 34,000 acres, including the Maverick, Kaufman, and Edwards counties' school land, but both the title and method of acquisition were soon challenged by the principal users, D. M. Devitt and C. H. Flato, who operated as the Mallet Land and Cattle Company. Devitt and Flato had moved cattle into Hockley County in the mid-1890s and were using approximately 74,000 acres when Slaughter's agents began soliciting the various counties for title. To curtail Slaughter's activity, Devitt filed lawsuits against him for control of the Maverick, Kaufman, and Edwards counties' school lands.

While Devitt's suit was pending in court, Slaughter sent W. E. Kaye to Eagle Pass to try to obtain title to the Zavala County tract that Devitt was using. On February 15, 1901, the commissioners court there granted Kaye the deed, and on the same day Slaughter's son-in-law, attorney G. G. Wright, won the Kaufman County suit. Optimistic over the double legal triumph, Slaughter predicted that Devitt and Flato would soon capitulate.

> With this deed in our hands, we will *at once* sue Mr. Devitt for "Trespass to try title," and there is no court on this earth that will keep us from possession of the land. With Kaufman, Maverick, and Zavala Counties in our possession, where is Devitt and Flato? They will be around soon for a compromise. Mark what I say, Flato will be over here soon, wanting to compromise and telling us how much he has always loved the Slaughters.

Most critical was the 17,712-acre Edwards County tract. It was in the center of Devitt's ranch, and its acquisition would assure Slaughter of a contiguous block. Without it his ranch would be divided by a ten-mile strip. Devitt, with holdings on both the north and south side, faced an identical situation. Whoever lost would have the expenses of extra fencing, additional windmills, more line camps, and other things. While the case was in litigation, the Edwards County commissioners, who had previously sold the land to Slaughter's agent W. E. Kaye, then sold the land to Devitt and Flato, completely disregarding the previous contract with Kaye. With both parties claiming title, the stage was set for a major fight.

While Slaughter and Devitt fought over land titles in court, a small-scale range war threatened to erupt between the cowboys of the two ranches. In 1903 Slaughter took possession of the tract following the expiration of Devitt's original grass lease and promptly fenced it. During the next three months, the barbed wire was cut at least six times. The Slaughter cowboys blamed the Mallet hands and prepared for action, one even getting a blister on his leg from wearing a gun for several weeks. George Slaughter reported to his father that "I think [the cowboy] thought he might be called to fight any time."

Following Slaughter's enclosure of the land, Devitt obtained an injunction against Slaughter's occupation, but the Colonel's cowboys refused to abandon the pasture until faced with a contempt of court threat. Finally, after a preliminary hearing in Lubbock, United States Circuit Court Judge Edward R. Meeks ruled on May 31, 1904, in favor of Devitt and Flato, declared a permanent injunction against Slaughter, and ordered him to pay court costs. Slaughter appealed, but the U.S. Court of Appeals in New Orleans upheld the lower court decision on October 2, 1905. He then considered appealing to the U.S. Supreme Court, but there is no evidence that he ever did.[4]

Slaughter made one additional effort to break the Mallet control of southwestern Hockley County. Sending agent Ben C. Taber to Snyder and Seymour, he attempted to buy the Scurry and Baylor counties' lands that Devitt was leasing. The commissioners court in each county, however, refused to budge from its commitment, despite a $26,000 bid. In Knox County, Taber was more successful. He obtained title to a tract that joined on the northwest the main body of Slaughter's land in Cochran County, a tract that had previously been leased by Huling and Slaughter. Taber also acquired Lipscomb County's 17,712 acres in June 1900.

In spite of legal battles, Oxsheer, his agents, and others by the spring of 1901 had gotten Slaughter deeds and leases to 297,000 acres, most of which lay in one contiguous block. That figure included two blocks of land later reclaimed by Coke and Midland counties. Several years after the ranch was established, a survey by W. D. Twichell indicated that Slaughter owned 246,699 acres. For this land the Colonel paid approximately $240,000 to the counties and $95,000 in bonuses to Oxsheer and others for a total cost of $1.36 per acre. He also leased additional acreage from neighbors and from Slaughter cowboys who had established homesteads adjacent to or near the new ranch. It had been accomplished by swift action; more leisurely efforts would have failed, for some of the commissioners courts would have refused to sell had they been aware of Slaughter's objective. Indeed, after learning of the intent, two counties refused to accept larger principal payments in order to prolong interest rates, and others tried to rescind their sales.

In 1898, when title to only a portion of the land had been obtained, Slaughter began operations on the new ranch. At first he referred to it as the Sir Bredwell and Ancient Briton divisions of the Long S, but after 1901 he viewed it as a separate entity and called it the Lazy S. The Lazy S brand (⌒) was placed on the animal's thigh rather than on the side, as was the practice on the Long S, and it was shorter than the older Slaughter brand.[5]

Once the ranch was established, Slaughter moved rapidly to make the new investment profitable. In the spring of 1898, he hired as foreman Hiley T. Boyd, a wiry young cowboy who had worked in Hockley County for five years and was well acquainted with the often unstable conditions of South Plains ranching. Riding over the acquired lands on horseback with his new foreman, Slaughter outlined his plans, suggested windmill and fence locations, herd management and grass control methods. Then as additional lands were obtained, the Colonel channeled his instructions to Boyd through son George, who became the manager. From his new headquarters at Roswell, George Slaughter thereafter managed the Running Water, the Slaughter Hereford Home, and the Lazy S.

Good water throughout the new ranch was as essential as grass for the projected twenty thousand head of breeding stock. Only a few wells, drilled by previous occupants and scattered over a thirty-mile area, dotted the arid landscape. Slaughter outfitted a crew and put it to drilling wells and erecting windmills. At twenty-one natural depressions and buffalo wallows selected by Slaughter and Boyd, the crew used a horse-drawn fresno scraper to dig sizable dirt tanks. To increase the flow of water, eighteen tanks were supplied by two windmills each and three were watered by three wells each. At the end of six years, the Lazy S had fifty-four windmills at twenty-four tanks, generally placed about five miles apart. By 1911 the investment in wells was nearly sixty thousand dollars. Such improvements were necessary, Slaughter

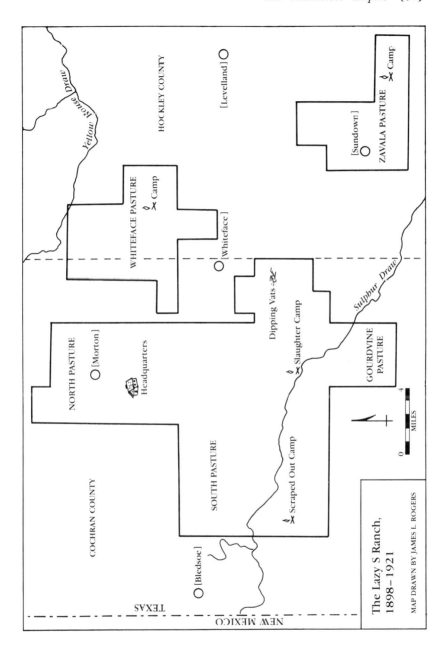

The Lazy S Ranch, 1898–1921

MAP DRAWN BY JAMES L. ROGERS

maintained. "We are blowing in a big lot of money up there on the plains and down in the Pecos valley," he wrote his manager in 1901, but "bearing in mind that it is simply foolishness to save the nickels and lose the Dollar, you will get through alright. On the other side look out for the dimes, and the Dollars will look out for themselves."[6]

As well drilling and fencing were completed, the Lazy S was stocked with the Cross-J Hereford herd and mixed-breed cattle from the Long S. Once completed Slaughter's empire took on a new dimension as his ranches now spread over two hundred miles of West Texas. Eager to promote his cattle business, he invited livestock journalists and others to tour the West Texas prairies with him. On his summer inspection in 1899, Slaughter was accompanied by H. W. Caylor, a Big Spring artist, who recounted the fourteen-day trip for the readers of the *Texas Stock and Farm Journal*. To travel over his ranches, Slaughter used a custom-built carriage. Similar to any army ambulance, the coach was equipped with a kitchen and cushioned seats that could be removed for a bed. Drawn by four matched mules, the rig bore paintings of Sir Bredwell and Ancient Briton on each side of the driver's seat.

Using the special coach, Slaughter and Caylor, accompanied by Bob Slaughter, visited all four divisions of the Long S range. First, they stopped at Rattlesnake, where three thousand shorthorn cattle were being rounded up. From there the party proceeded to the Sulphur pastures in Borden and Martin counties, then turned northwest, stopping briefly at the Buffalo division in southern Dawson County. At Indian Canyon, ten miles east of present-day Lamesa, the group rested briefly and then traveled north approximately twenty-four miles to the Tahoka Lake Ranch. From there, the entourage moved into Hockley County, where it visited what Slaughter called the Ancient Briton Wellbred Ranch, the future Lazy S. For a brief period, the Ancient Briton Ranch was headquartered at what later became the Whiteface Camp of the Lazy S Ranch. (The site was served by a unique two-story dugout, now preserved at Texas Tech Museum's Ranching Heritage Center.)

Caylor reported that the Ancient Briton Ranch was subdivided into three pastures, one each for the famous bulls, Ancient Briton, Hazel Dell, and Protection. After examining the Hereford herds in each pasture, the party proceeded northwest twenty-one miles (four miles northwest of present-day Morton) to the division where Sir Bredwell reigned supreme. There Caylor, greatly impressed, drew sketches for a life-sized oil painting of Sir Bredwell and made a highly favorable comment regarding the bull and the operation of the ranch.

> This is truly the greatest purebred Hereford herd in the world. . . . Everything on Col. Slaughter's ranches is conducted on the most systematic and scientific scale; so much that it would be impossible for one bull to get in another's pasture without immediate discovery, and the cows of each herd are counted daily, thus making his method equal to hand-breeding. The location is on a range which was never successfully developed until it came into Col. Slaughter's possession. Now it is one of the best watered-ranges in the country.[7]

Eager to continue to capitalize on such favorable publicity, Slaughter invited a reporter for *Farm and Ranch* magazine to accompany him on his 1900 summer tour. He followed the same route as with Caylor. This guest, also ecstatic with what he saw, reported that at Soda Springs, a few miles north of Sulphur, the steers were "so uniform . . . it seemed we were viewing the same individuals over and over again. This was the largest and finest bunch of beef cattle I have ever seen." At Tahoka Lake the reporter was impressed when Slaughter stopped to give lessons to a fencing crew. The tour ended at the Sir Bredwell division in Cochran County. Like Caylor, the unnamed reporter thought what he had seen was almost unbelievable. "In all the years I have been identified with the cattle industry in the North and East, I never for a moment fancied that such system and method could reach this high perfection on a ranch so large." He calculated the total acreage of the Long S and Lazy S at 1,373,000 acres, stocked with 54,500 head of cattle. The trip required seven days, including six nights camped out on Slaughter land.[8]

Adequate grass, an abundance of good water, the best purebred cattle, and favorable publicity all combined, however, were not enough to assure success. Slaughter fully realized that sound and efficient business practices suitable for such a vast empire were equally as essential. Until 1895 he had run his cattle business from a saddlebag (inventories, business ledgers, and accounting procedures were nonexistent), but the Panic of 1893 and the drought that followed forced him to keep more accurate records of expense and income. With the 1897–1899 purchases of additional land and cattle, he updated his business practices. In his Dallas office he put to work the first of his college-educated sons, E. Dick Slaughter. Having graduated from the University of Texas in 1895 with A.B. and LL.B. degrees, Dick did further study at the University of Chicago and at Washington and Lee University. Soon after beginning his duties as a bookkeeper and stenographer in July 1897 and much to the chagrin of his manager-brothers, George and Bob, Dick made a fact-finding business tour of the West Texas ranches. "Take him to your ranch," the Colonel ordered George, "and give him facts in regard to *all* matters pertaining to the ranch and its interests. Don't be fearful of giving him too many details, but give him all facts in a systematic way for our future guidance as our business has now grown to such large proportions [*sic*] that it is highly necessary to have notes for reference in black and white."[9]

After the creation of the Lazy S Ranch, Dick Slaughter's business influence became more pronounced. At his insistence Colonel Slaughter agreed to create the C. C. Slaughter Cattle Company, Incorporated, a family-owned corporation to control the Lazy S Ranch. In the preamble to the charter of the corporation, Colonel Slaughter outlined his intention that the ranch serve as a permanent insurance policy for his wife and nine children. He emphasized that the ranch was to serve as "an indivisible endowment" for his family: "the title shall not pass from my wife . . . and my children . . . so long as one of my children shall survive." He divided the stock into ten equal portions.

Slaughter then appointed himself and the four oldest boys to serve as the corporation's first directors. Since he always required his family to be home for the Christmas holidays, directors' meetings were scheduled in Dallas on the fourth Monday in December. At those meetings, in spite of his intent to create a family-controlled corporation, the Colonel virtually dictated policy. He single-handedly directed ranch procedures and, as late as 1909, readily vetoed decisions made by his sons.

Dick Slaughter was elated about the incorporation of the Lazy S. "Just as soon as the corporation is fully launched," he wrote brother George, "I want to begin keeping a full set of books, stock-holders Minute Book, Directors minute book, Ledger Journal, Day-book, etc. I am going to keep all this Company business entirely distinct and separate from the C. C. Slaughter business." Insisting that his brothers supply him with a "full, itemized correct and complete *INVENTORY* of everything conveyed to the C. C. SLAUGHTER CATTLE CO.," Dick Slaughter soon aggravated his easy-going manager-brothers.

"Nobody on earth but you can get it up," Dick pleaded with George about the inventory, "and you know that it is absolutely necessary to have it, and to have it as soon as you can make it up." Like his older sons, Colonel Slaughter could see little sense in Dick's insistence on an inventory, and as a result Dick was forced to solicit the inventory in secret. "I don't know whether or not [Colonel Slaughter] would raise an objection or not. . . . I know this inventory ought to be here at the office." Another family member was interested. In May 1902 G. G. Wright, a brother-in-law, asked George for the inventory, which he too wanted without the Colonel's knowledge. Both failed, however, to get an inventory until nine years later and then only after professional accountants had toured the ranch.[10]

Before long, however, the senior Slaughter began to mistrust his bookkeeper son. Less than a year after Dick joined the office staff, the Colonel began communicating with George confidentially through his own handwritten letters. By 1902, perhaps discouraged by his father's unwillingness to reorganize office matters, Dick had lost interest in the family business. "I am forcing Dick down to his books," Colonel Slaughter reported to George in October 1902. "I give him until the 1st of November to get matters straightened up, and if he does not do it, I am going to let him go and get someone else." In an effort to give his son greater responsibility, Slaughter placed Dick in charge of rentals in the Slaughter Building, a handsome six-story structure the Colonel had acquired for his offices.

The new duties did not end the problems with Dick. In June 1904, while his son was on an extended vacation, Slaughter discovered financial shortages which he attributed to Dick's mismanagement. "Wish he was at home," he noted to George. "He will have some explanations, I think." Four days later he instructed his managers to report directly to him and placed management of the Dallas office in the hands of his son-in-law G. G. Wright. On June 24 he explained the office adjustments to George. "Dick's administration for the last year is found short $5096.00 for which he has given his note and he made a full and frank acknowledgement. . . . It seems he cannot touch it [money] without using it."

The incident provoked the Colonel to reevaluate all his ranching and business procedures. In a strongly worded letter to George, he demanded that stricter accounting records be kept of expense and income. "I am going to have this office run and run right or not at all," he stated and then explained his new and complicated procedures. Dick was to work under the supervision of G. G. Wright at a salary of $100 per month. "He cannot live with anything less," his father noted. "He has to change his way of living."

From then on money collected in the Dallas office from building rents was turned over to the janitor, J. P. Wiley, perhaps the only one Colonel Slaughter could trust. Then Wiley was to hand the money to Slaughter's stenographer, who was to deposit it. C. C. Slaughter, Jr., the Colonel's next-to-youngest son, was to audit the stenographer's accounts. Slaughter placed the blame for the troubles on family jealousy and dissension. "There has been in our business too great a fear of one of our people telling on the other for fear they would get mad, and the consequence is that I am working for you all, and it appears that all of you, or some of you are pulling trying to keep us from doing anything for you."

George, and probably the other sons, promised his father that he would be a better businessman. "Rest assured I will do the best I can with everything," and then added, "Now don't get it in your head that your boys are trying to rob you. I know we all spend a lot—it costs to run a big outfit."

Dick, however, refused to abide by his father's mandate and left the family business. "Dick has no work yet, that I know of," the Colonel reported to George, "but he thinks he will get into an insurance office pretty soon. . . . I am sorry it comes to you like it does, and I know from experience how deep it reaches." Consequently, from 1904 to 1908, Dick Slaughter worked as general agent for Aetna Life Insurance Company and then organized a wholesale tire company. In 1911 he became vice-president of Mat Hahn Packing Company and in 1914 formed his own oil exploration firm. He did not return to active participation in direct management of Slaughter affairs until after the death of his father in 1919.[11]

Following Dick's dismissal, C. C. Slaughter, Jr., and G. G. Wright, who was married to Slaughter's second daughter, Dela, assumed more important roles in the family business. Young C. C., who at one time wanted to work on the ranches with his older brothers, had begun working as an auditor in his father's office soon after graduation from Baylor University in 1902. After a few months he entered a tailoring business in the Slaughter Building. Then after a short-lived career in an ill-fated buggy manufacturing company, he rejoined his father's staff as bookkeeper in 1910. Wright, who worked for many years in the Dallas office as attorney, was verbose and stiff in his dealings with his brother-in-law managers and added little smoothness to the office management, but he retained the Colonel's confidence.

The older Slaughter boys remained in the west. From his headquarters at Roswell, George Slaughter continued to manage the Lazy S, the Running Water, and the Hereford Home. There he established his own bank, the American National. Bob Slaughter managed the Long S from his home in Midland. Although Bob was more experienced as a cowman than George, his immaturity and ambitions would not allow him to settle into regular routines. Fast horses and, later, fast automobiles became his trademark, and his reputation as a hell-raiser became widespread in West Texas. Bob Slaughter was once described by an old ex-Slaughter cowboy, Joseph Good, as "the most individualistic man" he had ever known. Good related that once, while attending the 1893 World's Fair in Chicago, Bob received a wire from the Long S wagon boss advising the manager to return to the ranch immediately. Ten days later Bob returned. "Why didn't you come right away?" the wagon boss reportedly inquired. The reply: "I thought from what you wired that the outfit had gone to hell anyway and that I had just as well stay and have a good time as long as I could." With his expense account frequently overdrawn, Bob often stretched his father's patience but never lost his favor. "Bob is going to be hard to get into line," the father once complained to George, "but means well and will come up all right."

In spite of all the family diversity and a far-flung operation, C. C. Slaughter retained tight control over his business. On the range and through his correspondence, he listened to and gave advice to his managers, often heeding what they had to say, but he never failed to let them know that he was in control. From his Dallas office, he coordinated all ranch operations. Generally, his ranching methods worked well. Cattle born on both the Long S and Lazy S were held for two years on the Long S. Should additional finishing be required, the herds were moved to the Lazy S or Running Water for grazing and from there to railheads at Bovina or Hereford.[12]

For many years Slaughter maintained a semiannual visitation routine. Normally in June and October of each year, he toured the ranches by train and coach, usually spending eight days there. From Dallas he rode the Texas and Pacific to Big Spring, then drove over the ranches by coach, generally following the route previously noted when he escorted the livestock journalists. After concluding his tour at the Lazy S or Running Water, he proceeded by coach to Portales, New Mexico, where he returned to Dallas on the train by way of Amarillo. On the spring tour, Slaughter evaluated the condition of range and cattle and determined the placement of herds for summer grazing. He also observed spring roundups, made decisions whether to send cattle to market, and gave instructions on ranch improvement. On his fall tours, he supervised selection of cattle being sent to market, evaluated range prospects for winter pasturage, and inspected watering locations.

For many years Slaughter accompanied his cattle to market. From 1882 to 1898, he went by rail to Kansas City, St. Louis, Chicago, and on one occasion, at least, to Buffalo, New York, seeking the best price for his products. Normally, he arrived a week ahead of his shipment and, while waiting for his cattle to arrive, analyzed and observed market trends. He often remained in Chicago for three or four weeks. His shrewdness at market was rewarded. For twenty years he reportedly held the record for prices paid for grass-fed beef.

Slaughter also became well known for his tenacity as a trader and businessman. He always demanded strong contracts from his creditors. When dealing with a cattle buyer, he required the purchaser to place "faith" money in a special account, funds that would be forfeited to Slaughter should the buyer default. When financing a buyer's purchase, Slaughter required at least 10 percent interest. A typical Slaughter contract was one he signed with Fount Oxsheer in 1900. Slaughter loaned Oxsheer $30,000 for three years at 10 percent. Securing the note with much of Oxsheer's patented land, cattle, and future increase of his herd, Slaughter was in a position to foreclose on all the land and cattle should Oxsheer fail to meet his first payment of $8,500.

By 1900 Slaughter had become one of the great cattlemen of America. Years of droving, herding, buying, and selling had given him an uncanny eye for cattle conditions and needs. Unlike many others he profited from prolonged droughts and economic depressions through manipulation of cattle and land. He always maintained an optimistic spirit based on a simple philosophy. "Keep all your heifers and raise all the cattle you can," he advised a group of young cowboys in the mid-1880s; "there might be times when prices would be low, but they always come back."

Slaughter also understood buyer habits and knew how to sell in

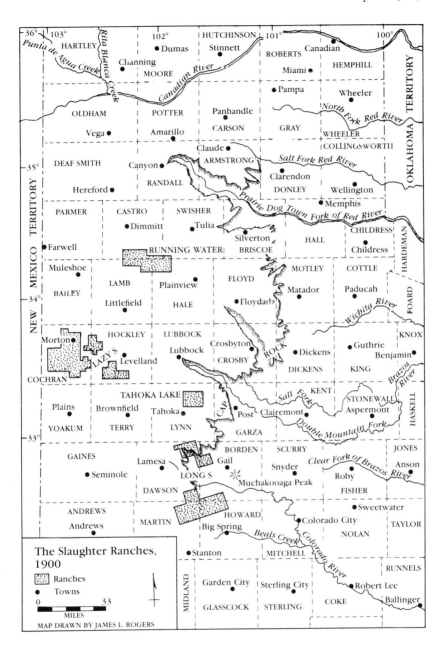

The Slaughter Ranches,
1900

Ranches
Towns

0   33
MILES
MAP DRAWN BY JAMES L. ROGERS

volume. "There is a good deal of difference between selling large numbers of cattle at a certain price and selling small numbers," he advised George on one occasion. "If you begin to distribute cattle in small numbers at a low price, the man learning this will offer a less price for large numbers." He also worked the market another way to his advantage. "It is not my idea to put much money in cutbacks," he explained to George about a herd of poor cattle, "but let them grow out till they get aged and slip them in with others on account of heft by age, so they will take them when they are heavy." Such methods obviously allowed him to get higher prices for low-quality beef.[13]

By the time Colonel Slaughter celebrated his seventieth birthday in 1906, his empire had reached its greatest height. He owned or controlled a million acres of West Texas, which made his business one of the largest individually controlled ranch operations in the nation. With herds numbering more than forty thousand head, all ranches were in full production, returning sizable profits to the longtime cattleman.

Slaughter's vast holdings enhanced his reputation. No meeting of cattlemen at the regional or national level was complete without a short comment by the legendary Slaughter. The Colonel often used such opportunities to bolster the Slaughter name, sometimes winning new friends with his pronouncements. For example, during a stormy meeting of the Cattle Raisers Association of Texas (formerly the Cattle Raisers Association of Northwest Texas) in March 1896, while debating qualifications for membership, Slaughter gave strong support to small ranchers. "A new member with two head of cattle . . . had just as much right as any other member to express his sentiments," Slaughter proclaimed during the argument.

At the 1906 Texas Cattle Raisers convention, Slaughter rose to the greatest height of his career. Meeting in Dallas, the association had asked the Colonel to give the keynote address on the subject, "The Passing of the Range, the Probable Extent of This Change, and Its Bearing on the Future of the Cattle Industry of Texas." Probably no man in Texas whose lifelong experiences were intertwined with the history of the range cattle industry was better qualified to discuss the topic.

Slaughter accepted the assignment with enthusiasm. As a result he delivered a forty-minute address in which he attempted to answer a question he had posed to himself many times, "What am I to do with my cattle if the range is taken from me?" His answer was his autobiography. He recounted his long association with the cattle ranges of the Southwest, particularly in West Texas. Revealing his love for the region, Slaughter described it for his fellow cattlemen as a "great table land country, beautiful to behold." There were two kinds of cowmen, the renters and the owners, he said. The renters did nothing to improve their stock and had little faith in the land. The owners, however, viewed the region in a different light, for they saw that, with improvements, the country would be the greatest cattle range on earth. Cattlemen, like himself, satisfied their hunger for land by buying it as best they could, from the state, from railroads, from counties that had four leagues, and from settlers. The cattlemen also improved their herds through crossbreeding and, as a result of their labors, Slaughter said, had made themselves wealthy men.

Slaughter gave credit to individual cattlemen, the cattle raisers' associations, and surprisingly to farmers for bringing civilization to North and West Texas. "The farmer will, in all probability, be a benefit to the cattle industry of the future. . . . [Steam tractors] are running now on your prairies, carrying from twelve to fourteen plows each . . . turning over many acres per day and doing it right. The farmer has learned how to manage his crops, and the stockman must learn how to manage his herds."

Slaughter concluded by correctly predicting that the Texas High Plains would eventually support both large cities and extensive cattle-feeding operations. "Look out for the future coming white city of the plains of Texas," he said. "I cannot say where it will be located, but someday you will see the greatest city . . . with teaming [*sic*] millions of happy, industrious people, railroads everywhere, all becoming cattle growers on a small scale."

Although Slaughter's optimistic nature prevailed in his address, he also recognized that his cattle empire faced immediate challenges from farmers. He well knew that, should he lose important lawsuits then in litigation, he would lose control of thousands of acres of land, which would in turn force him to dispose of his long established ranches. Thus, he shared with his audience his chief concern for the future of Texas cattlemen:

> The only trouble with this class of men [the big cattlemen] is that their range is being taken up in many places, by actual settlers and their cattle are disturbed, and they scarcely know whether to sell out at present prices, or run their cattle, believing if they do sell, they

will probably sit down in days to come and tell their sons they sold too cheap.[14]

Within two years of his statement, Slaughter had indeed decided to sell. What he did not realize was that his old, longtime enemies—depression, drought, and an agrarian-minded state legislature—would make his task of selling his ranches as difficult as trying to run them.

7

The Agrarian Challenge

While C. C. Slaughter was developing the Lazy S Ranch, his control of the older Long S was being challenged by agrarian interests. The Four-Section Act enabled land-hungry farmers to easily obtain title to large tracts; economic recovery on a national level, following the election of 1896, resulted in higher prices for agricultural commodities; and weather favorable for farming returned in 1895 to the plains. That year in Lubbock County, which lay between Slaughter's Long S and Running Water ranches, the vast IOA Ranch began selling its potentially rich agricultural lands to farmers. This gave the agrarians a solid foothold in formerly rancher-dominated West Texas.

Furthermore, the inventions which allowed cattlemen to make extensive use of the arid region worked similarly well for farmers. Windmills, which allowed ranchers to use pastures not watered by natural streams and lakes, made it possible for farmers to have water for domestic and stock use. Barbed wire likewise aided the farmers. If located in a big ranch pasture, farmers used fencing to protect their crops from a rancher's herd. Occasionally, they acquired control of watering sites long used by ranchers and enclosed them with barbed wire. To farmers in February 1901, Slaughter lost eight sections he had been leasing that included German Springs, the site of the ranch's original headquarters. Two Slaughter cowboys, who had secured title, secretly sold the land and disappeared. "It goes pretty hard on us, as we trusted these men," wrote Dick Slaughter to his brother George, "as they had been working for Bob a long time, and seemed to be honest. But such is life." [1]

For many years Slaughter and other West Texas cattlemen largely prevented farmer intrusion by perpetual leasing of state land. The increasingly farmer-oriented state legislature even prolonged their control in May 1897 with a major concession in an amendment to the Four-Section Act of 1895. Under that law, all lands, even those under lease, were subject to sale at any time. The new law of 1897, however, exempted leased lands from being sold south of a line extending from the northeast corner of Kent County on the east to the northwest corner of Yoakum County on the west. At the expiration of a lease, the land was subject to sale, but if there were no purchasers, it was available for leasing again by the original lessee. The land commissioner could cancel a lease only for nonpayment. Cattlemen, however, soon found a way, with the aid of the land commissioner, to circumvent the intent of the law. They canceled their leases before the expiration date and then re-leased for an extended time. As a result prospective buyers had no means of knowing when a tract was available. The practice became known as lapse leasing.

The exempted district included the Long S and the Tahoka Lake Ranch in Lynn County. There Slaughter freely used lapse leasing as a means to perpetuate his empire. In 1900 he worked out an agreement with Land Commissioner Charles Rogan to renew all his leases on enclosed land, then began to make additional improvements. As a further countermove, he persuaded the legislature to amend the lease laws again. The new law, which became effective April 19, 1901, provided that the lessee of school lands could not be disturbed in his possession during the term of his lease if he had placed certain improvements upon the property. Furthermore, the law specifically forbade the sale of leased lands until such leases had expired in twenty-one West Texas counties, including Lynn, Howard, Dawson, Borden, and Martin counties, those which encompassed Slaughter's major holdings. But leased lands in these counties would become subject for sale in 1906. This law and the practice of lapse leasing seemingly assured West Texas cattlemen perpetual control of public lands enclosed by their fences. C. C. Slaughter, whose wealth and influence may have been a major factor in the preferential treatment given to West Texas cattlemen, seemingly was in no danger of losing his leases. [2]

However, Slaughter's re-leasing practice was soon challenged in the courts. The decision was of major historic significance. East Texas farmer J. E. Ketner, who moved to the South Plains in 1900, waited for the lease on Slaughter's Tahoka Lake Ranch to expire. When he learned that Slaughter had renewed the lease prior to its expiration, Ketner filed suit in 1901 against the Texas land commissioner and Slaughter. Battle lines quickly formed, the ranchers, of course, rallying to the support of Slaughter and the farmers to the support of Ketner.

The case ultimately reached the state supreme court. Slaughter's son-in-law, attorney G. G. Wright, and Texas Attorney General C. K. Bell represented the ranchers' interest. Wright pressed the case on the issue that, because Slaughter had made improvements on the land, he was not to be disturbed until the leases expired. The court, however, saw the case in a different light; on June 9, 1902, it decided that the land commissioner did not have the power to cancel a lease for any reason other than nonpayment. Ruling that improvements were not the issue, the court indicated that since only the rancher (Slaughter) and the land commissioner were involved in the lease renewal, the new contract was unauthorized and illegal. Citing the law of 1895 regulating the sale and lease of school land, the court held that the intent of the law was for the land to be for sale, rather than for lease, at the termination of a lease and that the commissioner had no implied power to cancel a lease before its termination and to substitute another lease for a longer period. Thus, the second lease was invalid, and upon the expiration of the first lease, the land was subject to sale.[3]

Although the ruling affected only 22,000 acres of Slaughter's Tahoka Lake pasture, the decision had far-reaching implications. For many West Texas ranchers, it meant the ultimate loss of approximately half, possibly more, of land being grazed. With 200,000 acres under lease on his Long S Ranch, Slaughter knew that his big-ranch days were numbered. Since the court decision did not invalidate previous lapse leasing, however, he was, for the time being, still in the ranching business. "The old 'S' Ranch holds good for a while yet," he reported to George; ". . . I am not hurt quite as badly as I thought. It gives me more time to work. At the same time, every indication is that I will have to give up the old Long S Ranch."

Perplexed by the approaching loss of his old range, Slaughter considered several alternatives. He thought of converting his patented land into gigantic lots and feeding his cattle cottonseed meal. He considered sending son Bob to Arizona to see the Colonel's famous cousin

"Texas" John Slaughter, who could perhaps arrange for them to acquire a ranch in Mexico. He pondered the possibility of acquiring title to additional land and consolidating his holdings, or selling out entirely. Afraid that his favorite ranch, the Long S, would soon be gone, Slaughter decided to spend the summer of 1902 there.

While there he reached a decision. In collaboration with Bob Slaughter and bolstered with ideas from Wright, he determined to consolidate his holdings rather than sell his cattle. He concluded not to pay the state for leases and to let the land go on the market. Such action would hasten alienation of the land from the state. Once title passed to prospective settlers, Slaughter felt that he could purchase the land directly from the individuals who had bought it from the state. In doing so Slaughter planned to consolidate the Long S into a pasture twenty-one miles long and eight miles wide.

Slaughter's plan for retrenchment was threefold. First of all, he would reduce his cow herd by half. "I had rather have a little money out of the cattle than to have them throw their heels up to the skies next spring and have nothing," he said. Second, he would incorporate his personal holdings as the C. C. Slaughter Company. In doing so, he hoped to remove his land disputes from local courts to federal jurisdiction in order to get away from "local prejudice."

> Some counties, Borden, for instance are so prejudiced against me that I can get no more justice than a rabbit, and they cannot tell what they have against me either, more than I own some land and cattle in that vicinity; and they tell a man who has land and cattle to "go away back and sit down." So my idea is to get before the Federal Courts . . . and if they come it will cost them something, and I can tell them to "go away back and sit down," for I am going to get justice. Justice is all I want.

Third, he would place as many of his own men on the land as possible, and then he would buy other land from the actual settler. "What I want will cost me 250 to 300,000 dollars and don't know that I can reach. . . . This is high but will never be lower." If he could acquire title to the land, Slaughter would then have two large ranches of near equal size, the Long S and Lazy S, one each for his two managers.

Slaughter made two other important decisions for retrenchment. Knowing that he could no longer hold his leases on the Running Water Ranch, which lay north of the protected lease line, he would allow settlers to file on its public lands without harassment from him. Destined to become a rich agricultural area, Slaughter's patented Running Water holdings would rapidly increase in value. Then in October 1904, he sold his patented holdings, which encompassed Tahoka Lake in Lynn County, to Jack Alley, his longtime friend and employee.[4]

Slaughter's decisions precipitated a land rush to the plains. The land law of 1901 provided that a prospective settler could file on four sections of land if not more than two of them were classified as agricultural. It also stipulated that application for the purchase was to be filed with the clerk of the county in which the land was located (rather than in the General Land Office) and was to be accompanied by an affidavit that the applicant wanted the land for a home. The county clerk was required to receive the application, endorse it on the day and hour of filing, and record it without delay. Unfortunately, the law created havoc at several county seats as large leases expired. Cowboys lined up against farmers in shoving contests to see which group could file claims first. In one instance Slaughter produced his own group of "settlers." While on a trip to Big Spring, he made arrangements with attorneys there to locate prospective land seekers. To these persons he offered to pay filing fees, surveying expenses, and interest on loans until such time as the individual was ready to use the land, and secretly he let them know that he would ultimately buy the land.

The first land rush occurred on September 2, 1902. Two Slaughter cowboys, O. D. Holloway and W. S. Willis, decided to take advantage of Slaughter's offer and located lands in Dawson County on which to file. A week before the filing date, the two camped inside the courthouse at Big Spring (at that time, unorganized Dawson County was attached to Howard County). "Everything went fine for about a week," recalled Willis. "But four o'clock in the morning before the filing our range boss, John Joiner, learned that there were a large number of men coming from Scurry County to contest for filing on this land."

Bob Slaughter, however, was prepared for such an event. He rushed reinforcements to aid Holloway and Willis, supplying them with duck pants and leather belts. He ordered them to strip to the waist, put on the pants and belts, and then lock themselves together by holding on to the belts. One man, protected by the others, was to file the applications through a slot in the clerk's office door.

The expected contingent of trouble arrived at seven in the morning. Several tough-looking men entered the courthouse. Halted by the sheriff, they were searched and disarmed of "guns, some knives, and iron bolts," and were told that while the Slaughter men were not armed, they could be as rough as they wanted with their bare hands. Five minutes before the filing time, the newcomers rushed the Slaughter boys. But according to Willis, "it took two of them to hold one cowboy down. The boys made their filings."

A month later a second rush was staged at Big Spring. However, because there were too many prospective filers to camp inside the courthouse, the sheriff moved the men outside, stipulating that filing would be made at the clerk's window. The Slaughter cowboys promptly built a high-walled chute adjacent to the window. Their creation resembled a small fort, and during a rain storm, the enterprising cowboys simply covered the top to provide protection.

On the morning of October 2, a large group of Scurry County farmers arrived, this time armed. The cowboys, having been armed by Bob Slaughter, stood ready. The sheriff, acting to prevent bloodshed, promptly deputized twenty-five machinists from the nearby Texas and Pacific railroad shops and disarmed both groups. The farmers, deciding not to attack the solid wall of cowboys protecting the window, assaulted the courthouse door with sledge hammers. By the time they could gain entrance, however, the cowboys had filed their applications through the window. Bob Slaughter, flushed with victory, reported to his father that, through such tactics, he would get three out of every four sections originally leased.[5]

Other rushes followed. At Gail in Borden County, where cowboys and settlers adopted the practice of wearing red and blue ribbons on their arms as symbols of the side to which they belonged, as many as five hundred persons participated in some of the rushes. One of the biggest occurred in March 1903. The Slaughter cowboys, well experienced from the Big Spring rushes the previous fall, waited until five days before the filing date to arrive. About noon they rode on horseback into Gail, single-file. Jot Smyth, a Slaughter cowboy, vividly recalled the scene:

> The sheriff asked us what we were going to do and took our pocket knives. "Anybody that goes to fightin' goes to jail," he said. We went in and throwed these fellows out—just shoved them out the south door and we stayed there that night. The next morning they was comin' from every direction and they come in and threw us out, just like we did them. We came back the next day and pushed them out

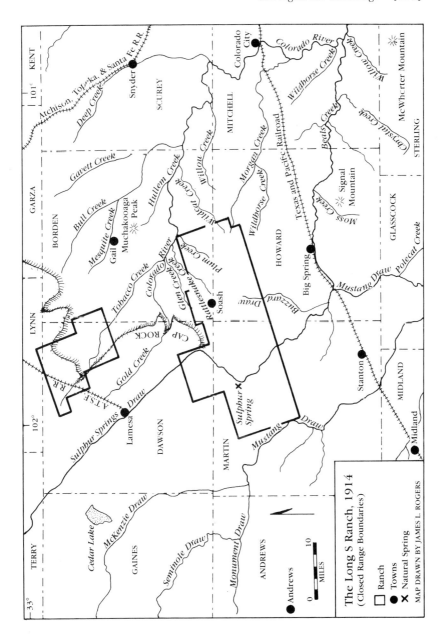

The Long S Ranch, 1914
(Closed Range Boundaries)

☐ Ranch
● Towns
✕ Natural Spring

MAP DRAWN BY JAMES L. ROGERS

again. They kept gettin' reinforcements and threw us out late the next afternoon and next day put in their filing.

While Slaughter's cowboys were losing the fight at Gail, vandals chopped down or damaged five windmills on the Long S. Disgruntled settlers also set fire to the prairie, forcing Slaughter to grade fireguards along the borders of his ranches.[6]

Such scenes were repeated throughout West Texas for the next three years. Finally, the legislature in May 1905 changed the land law, placing the sale of leased lands under the responsibility of the commissioner of the General Land Office, who was required to sell to the highest bidder. The reform not only ended the violent rushes but also considerably enriched the state treasury. Under competitive bidding the school fund received as much as twenty-five dollars an acre for land which, under the former law, brought in only a dollar and a half. It is not surprising that C. C. Slaughter, who in 1902 had noted that "this land is too high at $2.00 per acre," was no longer interested in purchasing land by bids. By 1905, however, he had acquired title to an additional 100,000 acres. Although the Long S was reduced in size to approximately 250,000 acres, most of it lay in two solid blocks in Dawson County and along Rattlesnake Creek in Howard and Borden counties. Slaughter's solidification of his holdings indicated the success of his retrenchment plan.

Throughout the lapse lease fight and land rushes, dry weather consistently plagued the South Plains. A hard winter followed by a dry spring in 1898 killed two thousand Long S cattle. The summer of 1903 was abnormally hot, and the following year brought little relief to Slaughter's pastures. In February 1905 he lost an undetermined number of cattle in a subzero winter storm. A month later, however, rain began to saturate West Texas. By September 24.64 inches of rain had fallen at Big Spring. The abundant precipitation, combined with the opening for sale of the formerly leased lands, created a boom period. "West Texas is this year flourishing," reported a Colorado City correspondent; ". . . grass has never been known to be so good; much better crops than ever known before. . . . Money is flowing, property is rapidly changing hands and population is coming in like the old boom days of '81 and '82."[7]

With the influx of new settlers into West Texas, Slaughter foresaw a ready market for his lands. "Range is finer than I have seen it since

1882," he wrote George in September. "It seems to me the time is not far distant when we will have to sell the land rather than run cattle on it." Such an idea, however, was painful to the aging cattleman. In December he noted caustically that it "seems Texas is pretty full of home seekers now, and it is to be hoped that if our cattle decrease in value, our land will increase and we can cut our ranches up and sell them, knock the cattle in the head, and ship the hides and their bones. However, I do not think it will come to that."

For ranchers the influx of large numbers of settlers increased problems. The destruction by settlers of grass and the increased competition for that remaining near railheads created difficulties for cattle shippers. The XIT, which owned its own private shipping pens at Bovina, closed the facilities to other ranchers in 1905, but Slaughter soon negotiated for continued use of the pens to ship Lazy S cattle. When Spade Ranch cattle belonging to Isaac Ellwood strayed into Slaughter's Lazy S pasture in Hockley County, Slaughter claimed a loss of almost $6,000 due to tick contamination. After Slaughter threatened suit, Ellwood paid $750 in damages. Settlers who moved into Slaughter's big pastures also presented a problem. Invariably, they fenced their land, forcing Slaughter to divide his pastures, often isolating portions of his lands. Before 1900, especially on the Running Water Ranch, Slaughter had compromised with farmers filing on school land by trading land in order to keep his own in one block.[8]

Even as early as 1900, while developing the Lazy S Ranch, Slaughter was willing to dispose of the Running Water at two dollars an acre, but since adjoining state land was available at the same price, he had few inquiries. Rumors of railroad construction in 1905 on the plains, however, rapidly fueled interest in his Running Water lands. In March the Colonel was approached by Charles K. Warren of Michigan, who wanted to enlarge his Muleshoe Ranch. In 1901 Warren had established the 40,000-acre Muleshoe Ranch in Bailey County; later purchases increased his holdings to 150,000 acres by 1907.

Sensing that prices were soon to rise sharply, Slaughter declined Warren's offer of approximately two dollars per acre. He acted wisely. In Plainview promoters speculated that the Santa Fe was soon to build its lines southward from Amarillo and northward from Coleman. Land values adjacent to or near the community rose rapidly, and by September 1905 property was selling for five to ten dollars an acre. Plainview boosters approached Slaughter for a contribution to a bonus to entice the Santa Fe, but he refused, convinced that the railroad would build there with or without his support.

The abundant rains of 1905 continued into the following year, and as a result Slaughter asked still higher prices for his land. In August 1906 he refused an offer of eight dollars an acre for a portion of the Running Water Ranch. "It is still raining down there," he wrote while vacationing in Wisconsin, "and land is going to sell." To exact the maximum possible from ambitious land speculators, in September 1906 Slaughter set the price of his Running Water land at ten dollars an acre but let it be known that he would negotiate with buyers who demonstrated their sincerity. While in Wisconsin, he was approached by a group interested in colonizing the Long S. To prospective buyers, he displayed his tough business disposition: if the group would place fifty thousand dollars in a Dallas bank as earnest money by October 1, then he would describe it. But he told George, "I don't expect to hear any more from them."[9]

He was, however, far more anxious to sell the Running Water Ranch than he intimated. A major prairie fire in March had burned through it, and the following December a severe snow storm killed one hundred head of cattle, primarily those, unable to drift with the storm, that piled up against barbed wire fences. First, though, he would promote the building of railroads into the ranchlands to stimulate increased settler interest and higher land prices. Santa Fe survey crews were already in the field. Avery Turner, vice-president and general manager of the Panhandle and Santa Fe, had approached Slaughter in May about right-of-way for a proposed "cutoff" to connect Santa Fe lines at Coleman and at Texico on the New Mexico–Texas border. Such a line would cut diagonally southeast to northwest across the South Plains, perhaps across the Running Water Ranch.

Slaughter refused to negotiate. His refusal may have doomed Plainview's opportunity to acquire the coveted Coleman cutoff. Instead, he talked to a group of Hereford promoters who were trying to link their city and Brownwood with a railroad to be known as the Panhandle Short Line. Since this line would pass through or near the Running Water, the Lazy S, and the Long S, in March 1907 he offered the company right-of-way, forty acres for a depot, and fifty thousand dollars, provided the road would bind itself not to put another depot nearer to his land than Dimmitt and to complete construction by May 1908.

The Panhandle Short Line, chartered March 30, 1907, and promoted by an "energetic, large, uncouth, and braggadocious" booster, J. H. Ransom, was soon the talk of the South Plains. Ransom, financed with funds secured from unsuspecting investors, pushed the grading but ran out of money before reaching Dimmitt. Refinanced in August 1907 by a group of Hereford businessmen and Slaughter, the Panhandle Short Line continued its promotional efforts. On August 31 George Slaughter, after meeting with sixty boosters in Lubbock, reported to his father that "they are very anxious for you to take the President of the road." [10]

Slaughter was flattered. During his fall tour of his ranches, he decided to view the proposed route. Accompanied by his wife and George, who provided his auto for the trip, he conferred with Hereford businessmen about the line. Then while passing through Lubbock, he told the *Avalanche* that he felt it was "absolutely necessary" that this route be built and that he was contemplating acting as president, provided he could get financier George Gould, Jay Gould's son, to buy the bonds. Capitalizing on such favorable publicity, the Panhandle Short Line quickly resumed grading.

Meanwhile, committees from Lubbock, Stanton, and Big Spring promoted their communities as potential route sites. Although Lubbock citizens did not raise money for this railroad, they dedicated a wide north-south strip through the city (present Avenue Q) as right-of-way for the Panhandle Short Line. Grading for the line continued as far south as Dimmitt (apparently financed with a portion of Slaughter's fifty-thousand-dollar pledge). However, a rival road, the West Texas and Northern, proposing to build along the same route as the Panhandle Short Line, began a survey from Stanton northward. Not certain which of the two routes to support, the communities involved almost ceased to make financial pledges to either.

By February 1908 West Texans became skeptical of the Panhandle Short Line scheme. Its promoters, Ransom and W. A. Squires, paid a final visit in April to Dimmitt, where they sold five thousand dollars in stock before going East "to make arrangements with the Chartered Construction Company to take the work in hand." Neither returned to the plains, and between Hereford and Dimmitt, Slaughter had a grade but no railroad. [11]

Meanwhile, unaware of the impending default and subsequent departure of the Panhandle Short Line promoters, Slaughter devoted some attention to another projected line, the Roswell and Eastern Railway. Begun in September 1907 by Houston promoter Edward Kennedy, this line was to extend from Roswell, New Mexico, to Lubbock, possibly through the heart of the Lazy S Ranch. As a resident of Roswell, George Slaughter promoted the line and pointed out to his father that Phelps White, manager of George W. Littlefield's LFD Ranch, which bordered the Lazy S on the northeast, was subscribing $10,000. "They have me down for the same amount," he reluctantly indicated. Promoters of the Roswell to Lubbock line told the Lubbock *Avalanche* that cereal king C. W. Post, who had purchased Fount Oxsheer's Diamond Ranch in Hockley County, was willing to subscribe $100,000 and that C. C. Slaughter had offered 100,000 acres of the Lazy S, "which would yield the railroad an estimated $2,500,000 five years after the construction of the road and would add $10,000,000 or $12,000,000 to the value of the entire Slaughter Ranch."

The Roswell and Eastern, like many other "paper" railroads, never developed beyond the talking stage. Its promoters, unable to secure strong financial backing, soon found themselves with no support at all as the established Santa Fe began its invasion of the South Plains. By February 18, 1907, that railroad had extended its tracks from Canyon to Plainview; then in December 1908, perhaps prompted by the potential competition of the Panhandle Short Line, the Santa Fe agreed to extend the Plainview branch an additional forty-five miles to Lubbock. There the line would eventually link via Slaton (in 1913) to the long proposed Coleman cutoff.

The Santa Fe had been besieged with requests from West Texas town promoters to place the new route through their communities. Influenced by C. W. Post, who had purchased the Curry Comb Ranch in Garza County southeast of Lubbock and who had paid the railroad a fifty-thousand-dollar bonus, the Santa Fe chose a route to extend from Coleman northwestward through Sweetwater, Snyder, Post City, and Slaton. Lubbock later profited from the route and replaced Plainview as the major trade center of the South Plains.[12]

With the extension of a railroad to Plainview, Slaughter realized that the appropriate time to sell Running Water land had arrived. Already he had been approached many times by prospective colonizers and salesmen, but none offered him an acceptable deal. In October 1906 he had noted to George that "lots of land dealers [are] following me, but . . . they all want to try and sell and get a commission, and that I will not do." A year later Slaughter suddenly changed his mind.

Fortunately, when he was ready to sell, a promoter made an offer he liked. Late in 1907 W. P. Soash, a thirty-five-year-old Iowa land dealer, came to his Dallas bank. Slaughter listened intently to the young man's plan and was charmed by his ingenuity, enthusiasm, and especially his experience. In 1903 Soash had begun selling Iowa real estate and, two years later, had founded the W. P. Soash Land Company. In his first venture he colonized a thirty-thousand-acre tract of the XIT Ranch northwest of Dalhart. There he established his first townsite, the little village of Ware, thirteen miles northwest of Dalhart on the Fort Worth and Denver railroad. Using first-class excursion trains designed to accommodate families from the Midwest, Soash was immediately successful. Business soon brought him into contact with Colonel Slaughter's brother W. B., president of the First National Bank of Dalhart.

W. B. ("Bill") Slaughter made arrangements for the young land promoter to visit C. C. Slaughter in Dallas. The two liked each other on sight. Slaughter decided that Soash's methods would work for the Running Water Ranch and accepted his offer of $10.50 per acre, or $900,000 for the entire ranch. "I think they [Soash and his partner, C. E. Larsen] are pushing fellows," Slaughter noted to George, "and I believe they will sell the ranch. . . . Should they make a success of it, I intend to turn them then on your ranch [the Lazy S] and let them see what they can do with that."

In February 1908 Soash ran his first excursion train to the Running Water. Elated with the response of his prospective buyers, he quickly bought his partner's interest and as a result renegotiated his contract with Slaughter. On March 2 the two agreed to a new deal: (1) Soash was to pay an additional fifty cents or eleven dollars an acre for the 89,000-acre ranch; (2) Slaughter forfeited his interest in gross profits (or losses); (3) at the conclusion of a sale, Slaughter was to receive two to three dollars per acre and was to carry the balance for seven years at 6 percent; (4) Slaughter retained an option on fifteen thousand acres of good land reserved to be sold last, should Soash default; and (5) Slaughter had free use of the range for one year. "I like this contract better than the other," Colonel Slaughter wrote George. "Brings us [a] square $11 and we have no part in the profit or loss. I think he will sell at least 40,000 acres. We will get $100,000 out of it." [13]

Soash worked quickly. He laid out the village of Olton on the route of the proposed Panhandle Short Line. The promise of a railroad and

Soash's excursion trains from the Midwest led to the rapid sale of Running Water land. Within the year Soash, with volume sales approaching one million dollars monthly, became the leading land dealer in the nation. By the end of 1908, more than half the Running Water had been sold, and Slaughter had banked more than eighty thousand dollars. Pleased with Soash's success, Slaughter encouraged the colonizer to make a deal with George W. Littlefield for the LFD Ranch, which lay south of the Running Water in Lamb County and adjacent to Slaughter's Lazy S Ranch. Littlefield, however, refused Soash's offer of three million dollars for his 300,000 acres. The Colonel then tried unsuccessfully to interest Soash in the Lazy S Ranch. But Soash had analyzed the soil there and found that much of the Lazy S's 246,000 acres was so sandy that farming would be difficult. "Says he does not think the time is now ripe," Slaughter reported to George, "think he has an impression from the people around Plainview . . . that it is too much of a sand bank." [14]

Instead, Soash wanted the lush and level prairies of the Long S. On January 27, 1909, he offered $12.70 an acre for 110,000 to 175,000 acres in Howard, Borden, Martin, and Dawson counties. The terms of the contract were similar to those for the sale of the Running Water: Slaughter was to receive $2.70 an acre upon delivery of the deed and an additional dollar per year for the next three years; the balance was to be spread over a ten-to-thirty-year period. Pleased with the sale but aware of a pitfall, Slaughter wrote George his misgivings. "There is one advantage in the contract for him, that is, he might sell the best land and leave the balance in my hands. This I do not think he will do at all unless he has a bad drouth and stops his sales."

The first few months of Long S colonization were profitable. In early March 1909, the first trainload of prospective settlers, some from as far as Minneapolis, arrived at Big Spring. From there they were transported by auto twenty miles north to Soash's community on the Howard-Borden county line, which he had proudly named Soash. By July 1909 the colonizer, with forty laborers, primarily employed by the Soash Development Company and headed by Bob Slaughter, had built an impressive little village. It included a two-story hotel, a garage to house thirty automobiles, and a fine brick bank building. Soash had plans for a flour mill, a cement block factory, a canning plant, and parks. Soon the city boasted electricity, a water works, a telegraph, a telephone exchange, and several businesses. Seemingly, it was poised to become the "red letter" city of West Texas. To show off the new town, on July 4, 1909, Soash staged a celebration which attracted more than two thousand persons. In an attractive brochure, he boasted of the rich opportunities afforded in the "Big Springs Ranch" country, with lakes, creeks, and "ample" rainfall.[15]

Unfortunately, the spring of 1909 turned dry. Although June rains brought some relief, by late summer prospective-settler visits were on the decline. As a further incentive to attract buyers, Soash joined Big Spring promoters in an effort to build a railroad from Big Spring to Lamesa, via Soash. This line, the Gulf, Soash, and Pacific, would intersect, it was hoped, with the Santa Fe's proposed line from Slaton to Lamesa. Soash then secured an agreement with the chief engineer of the Santa Fe, W. B. Storey, whereby the Santa Fe would absorb and complete his projected road, provided the city of Lamesa would move six miles east in order to lay on a more direct route. The citizens of Lamesa, however, refused to move, even after Soash threatened to build a new town on the proposed site. The continuing drought soon silenced his threat.

In spite of a large staff and a host of land agents, Soash could not sell Long S land; cancellation of existing contracts increased as the drought worsened. The spring and summer of 1910 brought no relief. Bob Slaughter reported that the drought was "worse than in 1886." Faced with bankruptcy, Soash turned to Slaughter for help. Fearing Soash's collapse would reflect badly on himself, Slaughter, in June 1910, reluctantly loaned him fifty thousand dollars and an additional amount in July. "The trouble is," the Colonel analyzed, "he went into several banks. Can't tell much about his business."

But relief from both Slaughter and July rains was not enough. His lines of credit closed, Soash was forced to begin liquidating assets. By the end of 1911, the lack of rain had ruined him, and in the summer of 1912, he closed his land company offices. Land unsold and abandoned by disgruntled drought-weary settlers reverted to Slaughter.[16]

Soash's initial success and subsequent failure made a major impact upon Slaughter's operation. The sale in 1908–1909 of Running Water and Long S lands and thousands of cattle gave the Colonel nearly $150,000 in cash. "I must get some of this money to work," he wrote George after the sale of the 1909 steer crop—his last major sale—"it will not do to let it stop."

The booming city of Dallas offered an excellent opportunity to put

the "money to work." He invested most of it in the Slaughter Building. For a number of years, Slaughter had occupied a three-story office
building on Main Street. In September 1902 he purchased the adjacent
National Exchange Bank Building, added two stories to his office, and
renamed the two remodeled structures the Slaughter Building. Then
in 1905, after the National Exchange Bank merged with and moved to
the American National Bank, Slaughter added a west wing. In 1909,
with surplus money from the sale of land and cattle, he completely
renovated his original offices and added three stories to the entire structure, which became an imposing addition to the Dallas skyline. Designed by Chicago architect Clarence Bulger in Romanesque style, the
building was "one of the most incredible and unique hybrids in the
history of American architecture."

Slaughter also found another Dallas site attractive. In December
1908 he purchased a piece of downtown property for $29,000 and in
June 1909 acquired an additional seventy-five feet of frontage on Elm
Street for $100,000. "I think this city is the best place to put our
money," he wrote George in defense of his actions. "Dallas now has
100,000 people, and is booming right along." Slaughter continued to
purchase Dallas real estate, and by the time of his death in 1919, his
holdings included approximately thirty pieces of property in that city
and its vicinity, including nearly one thousand front feet of prime downtown Dallas.[17]

When Slaughter decided to allow W. P. Soash to sell his ranches,
he incorrectly presumed that his cattle-ranching days were over. Soash's
failure to dispose of all the land, however, left him with approximately
200,000 acres of the Long S in terrible disrepair. Bob Slaughter, who
had managed the ranch since 1888, had allowed cattle, fences, and
watering places to deteriorate. Bob had been distracted first by the
land rushes and later by the colonization efforts. His mismanagement
had angered his father several times; however, always partial to his second son, Slaughter usually turned his back on Bob's inability to manage the ranch.[18]

In 1911, however, when it became obvious that the Colonel would
regain the use of the Long S, he asked his longtime friend and employee, Jack Alley, to take over its management. Alley, who had previously managed the Tahoka Lake Ranch, resigned as postmaster of
Tahoka to take the Long S job. He immediately launched a series of
improvements. First, he persuaded Slaughter to acquire additional

land with good water and to drill more wells on the Long S, which had
been relying primarily on live water streams and tanks. By creating
additional watering places, Alley felt he could more efficiently utilize
the grass. From 1912 to 1915, he drilled twenty-five wells with windmills to serve four thousand cattle and restored the Long S to its former
position as a profitable ranch. Thereafter, the delighted owner spent
the summers at the ranch's headquarters at Soash.

The instability on the Long S during the Soash years was offset by
George's sound and stable management of the other ranches. From his
Roswell office, George efficiently managed the Lazy S, the Running
Water, and the Hereford Home, a greater investment than the Long S.
From 1898 to 1910, George had handled more than a million dollars
worth of land, cattle, and supplies. In addition, in 1906 he established
the American National Bank in Roswell and made it financially strong.

Although his confidence in George continued to grow, there is no
record that Slaughter lauded his son's efficient management until after
the lapse of nearly twenty years. "I do not see where you have made any
mistakes and that is saying quite a great deal," he wrote in 1909, "for
when we look back and do not find any bad mistakes, we are bound to
say that it is well-managed, so I told you to go ahead and do what you
thought best and it could be all right with me."

On the other hand, Slaughter was extremely reluctant to turn control of any of his business over to his other sons. Dick, Alex, and C. C.,
Jr., had all worked for their father and engaged in other business enter-
prises, but they had failed to make any money. By 1910 the younger
brothers were insisting that they be allowed to assume management of
the "company" ranch, the Lazy S. In February 1910 their father finally
relented. "We are trying to get things straightened out the best we can
and come under a straight organic law according to corporation laws,"
the Colonel wrote George. "This is going to seem unnecessary to you
at first, as I have always thought it was, but you must bear with it and
you must bear with the other officers and directory. They may pass
some rules that will seem to you unnecessary, but you must bear with
them." Even though they had elected officers to handle the C. C.
Slaughter Cattle Company business, for a year and a half Slaughter
ramrodded his will over that of his younger sons. "We had some little
ups and downs," he wrote George following one particularly stormy
meeting. "A great many resolutions were proposed that I really vetoed.
Thought it was unnecessary. Of course that looked like I was going

against the directory, and told them we could not admit of any scheme being worked. . . . We had some rows, but did not amount to anything, and I hope has passed over." [19]

Even at the age of seventy-four, Slaughter probably would not have relinquished control of his holdings had it not been for a serious accident. In August 1910, while vacationing at the Resthaven Hotel in Waukesha, Wisconsin, he fell and broke his hip. [20] The injury left him crippled for the rest of his life. About the same time, his failing eyesight impaired his ability to conduct daily business. As a result C. C. Slaughter turned the management of his cattle interests over to George Slaughter and allowed his sons to assume responsibility for the Lazy S on condition that George should remain the manager and also the manager of the Long S with Jack Alley as the resident supervisor. The Dallas and vicinity real estate affairs were turned over to son-in-law G. G. Wright and other members of the family.

Although his retirement ended his active role in the management of the cattle business, Slaughter, through Jack Alley, kept in close contact with it. But most important, retirement from business allowed him to devote time and money to his favorite charitable interests. Sometimes quietly but usually boisterously, he had over the years created another kind of empire of religious and medical institutions that wore the Slaughter brand—an empire, he hoped, that would survive him and perpetuate the Slaughter name.

8

Banks, Baptists, and the Legacy

Throughout his career, Colonel Slaughter dedicated most of his time to the cattle business. Three other interests, however, attracted his attention, and to these he wholeheartedly devoted himself when presented the opportunity. They were his beloved city of Dallas, his church, and his family.

When Slaughter moved his family to Dallas in 1873, the community boasted a population of 7,054; at his death in 1919, it had 150,000 residents. Over the years his love for the city grew as rapidly as its population. He admired its busy atmosphere, its steady growth, and its abundant opportunity. In addition to his heavy investment in city property, he helped promote numerous businesses, major civic events, churches, and medical institutions.

Slaughter monitored Dallas' financial, social, and philanthropic activities through his long association with the city's banks. Following his organization of the American National Bank on March 4, 1884 (see chapter 3), Slaughter served as its vice-president but rarely participated in the bank's daily business activity. Primarily tending to his own affairs, he left banking to the bankers. It was, however, a profitable venture, paying Slaughter an average 12 percent annual return on his investment. Only when the American National merged in June 1905 with the National Exchange to become the American Exchange National Bank did he become dissatisfied with the bank's operation. "Since my return home," he noted to George, "there has been many transactions that have transpired, some of which I do not altogether approve. . . . I refer to the selling out, as I call it, of the American National Bank." Unhappy because he lost controlling interest in the bank and a good tenant in his building, Slaughter considered blocking the transaction:

> [E.J.] Gannon and [J.B.] Wilson . . . were by some means persuaded (how and by what I will have to learn) to sell out the stock. . . . While I could have broken the trade, I would have been in a worse condition then [*sic*] to let it go on, as I would have had to take charge of the bank myself.

However, Slaughter consented to the merger, and for his $30,000 investment in the old bank, he received $150,000 with an option to buy into the new bank. In October 1905 he invested $50,000 in the American Exchange National and became a director and vice-president, positions he held until his death.

The merger created a powerful financial institution in Dallas, and by 1910 the bank was the state's largest, with capital and surplus totaling $2,500,000. Subsequently, the American Exchange merged in 1929 with its major rival, the City National Bank, thereby creating the powerful First National Bank. The consolidation reunited the banking lineages of two former cattlemen bankers, Slaughter and William E. Hughes, who had dissolved partnership in 1879.[1]

Perhaps Slaughter's greatest civic contribution to Dallas was his service as president of the Confederate Veterans Reunion Association. In June 1901 the United Confederate Veterans in their annual convention at Memphis, Tennessee, chose Dallas as their next reunion site. A month later Dallas civic leaders named C. C. Slaughter chairman of the local arrangements committee for the reunion. Slaughter enthusiastically accepted the responsibility, obtained a charter for his committee (the Texas Reunion Association), and became its first president. The new organization set its goals; it was to entertain the ex-Confederates royally, to preserve historical and biographical matter pertaining to Texans who had served in the Civil War, and to erect a statue of Robert E. Lee in Austin.

After months of preparation, on April 22–25, 1902, Dallas hosted ten thousand veterans and "80,000 to 200,000" visitors, the former figure probably being the more accurate. The reunion, reportedly "the greatest gathering of people ever held in Texas," consumed 41,500 pounds of meat, 20,000 pounds of potatoes, and used hundreds of tents and beds at a cost to the Texas Reunion Association in excess of $58,000. Following the convention, highlighted by a visit from Mustafa Ben Selim, the caliph of Bagdad, accolades came from throughout the South. As chairman Slaughter was lauded for his "herculean" effort. According to a Dallas reporter, "his shoulder has been close to the wheel at all times and some day the people of Texas will more fully appreciate the magnitude of his labors." In spite of his hard work, Slaughter apparently did not pursue the interests of the Confederate Veterans Reunion following the Dallas convention.[2]

C. C. Slaughter made a more important contribution to religious activities. A longtime member the First Baptist Church of Dallas, he served on the 1890 building committee that supervised the construction of the church's present sanctuary. Of the $90,940 cost, he reportedly contributed $60,000, or about two-thirds of the total.

As his wealth increased, Slaughter became a favorite target for fund-seeking Baptist leaders. In 1896 he was persuaded to contribute $5,000 to Baylor University. As a result he was approached in August 1897 by Baylor's financial manager, J. M. Carroll, about an even larger contribution. While Slaughter was vacationing in South Dakota, Carroll spent three days laying before him a plan to eliminate the combined $200,000 debt of seven Texas Baptist schools. He asked Slaughter for an initial donation of $50,000. "He made no answer then," remembered Carroll. "Finally, Colonel Slaughter arose, took my hand, and said, as nearly as I can remember, these exact words: 'Jim, you go to your room and pray and I will go to my room and pray, and tomorrow morning I will give you my answer.'"

Unknown to Carroll, Slaughter had financial problems. The previous May he had spent $50,000 for the Goodnight Hereford herd and, while en route to South Dakota, another $50,000 for fine Hereford bulls. To raise immediately still another $50,000 would be difficult, but the next morning he offered half the sum. However, he suggested that his money be used as a challenge grant. If donations from others lagged, Slaughter promised to provide future "stimulation." Then the two apparently agreed to stage a dramatic presentation at the fall Texas Baptist General Convention.

Carroll hastened back to Texas. On September 15 he met with representatives from four of the concerned schools and created the framework for the organization of the Texas Baptist Education Commission. Participating in the initial plan were Baylor University, Baylor Female College at Belton, Howard Payne College at Brownwood, Decatur Baptist College, and the East Texas Baptist Institute at Rusk. Burleson College at Greenville and Simmons College at Abilene chose not to join.

Then on November 8 before fifteen hundred delegates to the Baptist convention at San Antonio, Carroll outlined his plan for the consolidation of the indebtedness and the coordination of activity of the Texas Baptist schools. At the conclusion of the presentation, Slaughter dramatically rose and stated that he would donate $25,000. The announcement did its work. The stunned convention not only adopted the plan but also immediately subscribed $7,000 to retire a pressing indebtedness at North Texas Baptist College at Decatur. And Slaughter's announcement stimulated additional support. Four years later the Baptist Education Commission reported that $211,251.51 had been subscribed for the five participating colleges, enough to eliminate their indebtedness. Slaughter had given $37,000 of that amount.[3]

In addition to solidifying Baptist education in Texas, Slaughter's contributions created widespread favorable publicity which bolstered both his banking and cattle businesses. No one did more to stir Slaughter's heart—and open his checkbook—than George Washington Truett, a dynamic young Baptist preacher who became Slaughter's pastor at Dallas in September 1897. Through subtle appeals to his pride and vanity, Truett gained Slaughter's financial support of Baptist work. In May 1903 he influenced Slaughter to pledge $50,000 toward a new Baptist hospital. Constructed on a site where the Colonel had once bedded down cattle, the hospital opened in March 1904. Reportedly, the directors considered naming the facility in honor of its generous benefactor, "but the disadvantages of having a hospital known as the Slaughter Hospital brought the decision to find a less pointed name," the Texas Baptist Memorial Sanitarium.

The hospital became the Colonel's favorite charity. He worked hard in its behalf, personally soliciting money for its support. In April 1907 he obtained, on his own security, a $50,000 loan for the hospital, a note he would later forgive. From November 1908 to May 1911, he served as president of the board and, in this capacity, in October 1909 supervised the opening of the sanatorium's handsome new five-story building.

In November 1913, encouraged by Truett, Slaughter once again stunned Texans by pledging a challenge gift of $200,000 to the hospital. In a letter Truett read to the Baptist General Convention, philanthropist Slaughter promised to give two dollars for every three given by others in a drive to meet the "remarkable growth and urgent needs" of the sanatorium. Although the hospital failed to raise the $300,000 necessary to claim his total offer, the Colonel made a donation at the ratio he had promised.

In June 1918 Truett, for his last time, appealed to Slaughter for a financial donation for the sanatorium. Shortly before leaving to spend six months with the United States Army in Europe, he persuaded Slaughter to cancel $162,000 he held in the hospital's bonds. According to J. B. Cranfill, the resulting cancellation of the bonded indebtedness was "the crowning achievement of C. C. Slaughter's life." The Colonel's total contributions to the sanatorium, which was renamed Baylor Hospital in 1920, may have exceeded $320,000.[4]

Truett also persuaded Slaughter to donate to two other Baptist causes. In November 1912 at the annual state Baptist General Convention, meeting at Waco, the Dallas pastor announced that Colonel Slaughter had pledged $50,000 to Baylor University's endowment fund. Once again, it seemed to a Waco reporter, "the incident . . . swept the audience like wild-fire. . . . A mighty cheer was given, and it was some time before order was restored, following the joyful announcement." Using the announcement as a catalyst, Truett promptly secured additional pledges of $120,000.

Truett's straightforward manipulation of Slaughter probably accounted for the Dallas minister's repeated success with the cattleman. A letter from the pastor to the philanthropist, written on Sunday morning, January 16, 1916, reveals Truett's diplomacy and careful timing. ". . . as I go more deeply into the subject of how we may best help the great Education Cause, in which we both are so vitally interested," he wrote, "and especially in view of the incomparable and unrivalled place of leadership you have so long held among Texas Baptists, I am venturing to make this suggestion to you: If you can start this campaign with Ten Thousand Dollars, I will see to it that half of your gift may be paid on the last day of this brief campaign . . . and the other half later in the year." Truett explained that the timing of Slaughter's payment "would not be for the public, but for the little group that ought to know, and the public would be concerned only with the gloriously inspiring fact of the gift itself."

Promising that the announcement of Slaughter's gift during the Sunday morning service "and in all the Texas dailies tomorrow" would allow Truett "to make inspiring use of it," the pastor suggested that Slaughter "simply send me a card to the pulpit when you come to church this morning, saying in a line that you will start the campaign with Ten Thousand." In a carefully worded postscript Truett added that one of the "bretheren" had phoned that, after having "thought and prayed much," he would give $5,000 to the cause. Not one to be out-given, Slaughter complied with Truett's request. Upon arriving at church, he sent his answer in a note to the pulpit. "Believing in your cause and praying for your success, showing my faith by my works, I will open your campaign by a gift of $10,000." An announcement to the effect appeared, as promised, in Monday's newspaper.[5]

Considering his involvement in an unhappy conflict within Texas Baptist circles, Slaughter's munificent contributions were remarkable. As a result of a dispute between two Baptist newspaper editors, S. A. Hayden and J. B. Cranfill, Slaughter was drawn into an argument which produced seven years of court litigation. As editor of the *Texas Baptist and Herald*, Hayden had been criticizing Texas Baptist leaders for many years, particularly those on the Baptist Mission Board located in Dallas. In response, the board lashed back at Hayden and attempted to disqualify him as a delegate to the October 1896 general convention at Houston. The convention approved a compromise resolution which censured but did not unseat Hayden.

Meanwhile, J. B. Cranfill, editor of the moderate *Baptist Standard*, defended the Mission Board. The Houston debate was continued in the editorial columns of the two rival Baptist newspapers, and as a result more than twelve hundred messengers, or delegates, gathered at the San Antonio convention in November 1897. The Mission Board of the Baptist General Convention again recommended that Hayden be excluded because of his "ceaseless and hurtful war upon the plans, policies, work, and workers of his convention" and because "he is a breeder of strife and contention." As a personal friend to members of the Mission Board, Slaughter apparently supported Hayden's exclusion. Reportedly, he told an old acquaintance at the convention that "we are determined to down that man, S. A. Hayden." The convention voted 582 to 102 in favor of the board's recommendation.

Meanwhile, Slaughter angered Hayden even more when in December 1897 he bought half-interest in Cranfill's *Baptist Standard*.

Slaughter agreed to lend the enterprise $2,500 for working capital and stipulated that the paper move its headquarters from Waco back to Dallas. An elated Cranfill, who had gained a national reputation as candidate for vice-president of the United States on the 1892 Prohibition party ticket, responded in May 1898 at Norfolk, Virginia, by getting Slaughter elected first vice-president of the Southern Baptist Convention.[6]

Hayden, however, was not impressed with Slaughter's involvement. On April 28, 1898, he filed a $100,000 libel suit against the editor of the *Baptist Standard* and thirty other Texas Baptists, including J. M. Carroll, George W. Truett, and C. C. Slaughter. At first the defendants regarded the suit lightly. In a letter to his son George, the Colonel casually noted that he and his Baptist colleagues were being sued by Hayden simply "for interfering with his peace of mind, causing him to lose sleep, white-wash his hair, and racking his nerves." Hayden, however, pursued the suit seriously, and after four long trials, three appeals, and seven years of litigation, Slaughter did also.

The first trial jury in 1899 awarded Hayden $30,000 in damages, but in February 1900 the Texas Court of Civil Appeals ruled that the lower court had erred on several counts and sent the case back for retrial. The second trial, begun in February 1901, resulted in a mistrial.

A third trial began on June 17, 1901. Hayden's attorney placed Henry Evans on the witness stand. Evans claimed that Slaughter had told him at San Antonio that "we are determined to down that man S. A. Hayden." Slaughter responded by swearing that he had never made such a statement and that he had never seen or heard of Henry Evans. After two months of testimony, the trial ended in a second hung jury.

Before the fourth trial began, Hayden gathered evidence which showed that Slaughter and a Henry Evans had been schoolmates at Palo Pinto and were therefore old acquaintances. Faced with possible perjury charges and obviously wearied of the ordeal, Slaughter had his attorney, G. G. Wright, negotiate a settlement independently. It cost him $7,500.[7]

Meanwhile, the case continued through a fourth trial in which the jury awarded Hayden $15,000 in damages. The remaining defendants again appealed. On May 12, 1904, the Texas Supreme Court reversed the decision, citing error of the lower court. On the same day, an elated Cranfill and a disappointed Hayden boarded the same train at Dallas to attend the Southern Baptist Convention. When the two Baptist leaders met, both drew guns and fired. Miraculously, neither was hurt. Embarrassed by his own actions, Cranfill resigned as editor of the *Baptist Standard* and sold his interest in it. As Hayden's attorneys prepared for a fifth trial, Cranfill in April 1905 finally moved to settle out of court and subsequently paid Hayden $300 in damages and $6,000 in court costs.[8]

In the midst of the affair, Cranfill was asked whether the lengthy litigation was making Slaughter "soured" of his Baptist work. In his November 5, 1899, weekly editorial, Cranfill replied to the contrary. "[Colonel Slaughter] is not that kind of man. The man who engages in works of Christian beneficence because he loves God will get no more soured and discouraged on account of our difficulties in Texas than was Zorobabel [Zerubbabel] when under the lead of God he was rebuilding the temple at Jerusalem."

Cranfill's assessment was accurate. Slaughter continued to support Baptist work wholeheartedly. In addition to his term as vice-president of the Southern Baptist Convention, he served from 1897 to 1903 as president of the state Mission Board and from 1898 to 1911 as an executive board member of the Baptist General Convention of Texas.

In spite of his unhappy experience with Hayden, Slaughter remained deeply devoted to his faith. "We must try to live up to the mandates of the Bible," he once wrote George. "It is one of the greatest things we can have, that pearl of great price, and it is the gift of God, but he turns no one away who asks in faith, believing in His son."

Slaughter's continuing generosity toward Baptists was probably a severe disappointment to several of his children. Even levelheaded George complained, at least on one occasion. "I see they had to get you to raise the money for the trinity," he chided his father in May 1905. "Whenever they want money they call on C.C.S. and it generally comes." Perhaps embarrassed over his generous donations at the expense of his children, Slaughter in May 1909 sent all nine ten thousand dollars each. The gift, however, was not without attached strings. "I request that you let me hear from you one year from today, as to benefits received and financial condition of this gift at that time," he wrote. "I ask this in order that I may . . . [know] whether or not it is in hands competent to handle money."[9]

In such a manner, Colonel Slaughter dominated his children's lives until his death. Three of them, Dick, C. C., Jr., and Alex, lived in elegant houses built across the street from the Slaughter mansion on Worth Street. Following his hip injury in 1910, he often sat on a second-story veranda and with binoculars watched their family activities. On Sundays and holidays, especially Christmas, he demanded that his children and grandchildren (he was to have seventeen) gather at his spacious home. On such occasions twenty-five or more were often present.

Slaughter's closest personal relationship was with his eldest son George. Their correspondence with one another reveals common understanding, values, and mutual confidence. They rarely disagreed. When George died unexpectedly on July 15, 1915, at the age of fifty-four, a shattered Colonel Slaughter lost his most trusted adviser.[10]

Toward the rest of his family, Slaughter assumed a traditional patriarchal position. He employed all his sons, found prominent positions for his sons-in-law, and educated his daughters in eastern schools. Only when he became crippled in 1910 did he relax his control over his business operations and family affairs.

The Slaughter family often vacationed together. Traveling extensively, Colonel Slaughter and various members of the family attended world fairs at Chicago, St. Louis, and New York. They also regularly visited bath resorts at Hot Springs and Eureka Springs, Arkansas. Slaughter, who smoked small cigars, believed hot mineral baths helped to "boil out the nickotine [*sic*]" in his body.

In spite of his broken hip, Slaughter amazed his acquaintances by taking long automobile trips with his family. In June 1912, accompanied by his wife, his nurse, his chauffeur, his daughter Minnie and her husband, Dr. George Veal, C. C. Slaughter, Jr., and his wife, Elma, and their baby, Anella, in two Pierce-Arrow automobiles, he left Dallas for the West Coast. The Colonel's car, a Landau, modified similarly to his old horse-drawn ambulance, contained a bathroom and seats that could be converted into a bed. After touring his West Texas ranches, the Slaughters leisurely drove through Lubbock, Amarillo, Raton Pass, Pueblo (where they spent a week with W. B. Slaughter), Colorado Springs, Denver, Salt Lake City, Reno, Lake Tahoe, San Francisco, Los Angeles, San Diego, Yuma, Phoenix, Socorro, and back to Dallas by way of Colorado City. The trip, some 8,500 miles, required five months.

Pleased with the experience, Slaughter planned a similar trip for 1913. On June 5, with principally the same group in the same two cars as the year before, he left Dallas en route for New England to visit

Mrs. Slaughter's relatives and birthplace. Driving first by way of Houston to Galveston, the Slaughters sailed to New York. From there they drove to Philadelphia, Atlantic City, and New England, returning home by way of Buffalo, Cleveland, Chicago, Kansas City, Des Moines, Emporia (Mrs. Slaughter's former home), Wichita, Lawton, and Fort Worth. They covered seven thousand miles in five months.[11]

Rejuvenated by the extensive trips, Slaughter launched an ambitious but ill-fated project in 1914. While in Pueblo on the 1912 western tour, he apparently had visited at length with his brother W. B., who had established banks in Dalhart, Texline, and Pueblo, about C. C.'s idea to establish a trust company in the Southwest. This business, Slaughter theorized, would function as a banker's bank and as a loan company to serve major business financial needs in the Southwest. W. B. was elated with the idea; he moved to Dallas in 1913, assumed control of a small Fort Worth investment company, moved it to Dallas, and laid plans for a major stock subscription. From September 1913 to January 1914, he enlisted the financial support of all of C. C.'s sons (except E. Dick) and sons-in-law, each of whom signed notes for $11,000. Colonel Slaughter subscribed $50,000 and loaned the company an additional $20,000. Then W. B. and C. C. contacted other prominent southwestern cattlemen, inviting them to take stock and become directors of the new company. Among those who responded favorably were stock raisers Tom B. Burnett, R. S. Dalton, Jourdan Campbell, Sam Webb, W. L. Ellwood, John Scharbauer, and J. M. Cowden and lumbermen F. W. Foxworth and Cicero Smith.

In June 1914 W. B. Slaughter announced the formation of Bankers' Trust Company. It would have a capital stock of $5,000,000 and would deal in all aspects of finance except commercial banking. However, in spite of an impressive list of directors, the new company's business affairs were quickly criticized by Hutchinson and Smith, Colonel Slaughter's accountants. Questioning the issuance of a $20,000 stock dividend based on inflated bookkeeping procedures, the accountants pointed out to Colonel Slaughter and the other directors of the company that such a practice may have been illegal and that "great difficulty and serious delays were caused by confused condition of accounting and disappearance of so many vouchers."

Before company president W. B. Slaughter could explain the problem, events in distant Pueblo created even more difficulties. The Mercantile National Bank there, of which W. B. was president, suddenly closed on March 29, 1915. W. B.'s son, Coney, who was the bank's cashier, fled to Chicago but was later arrested and convicted of embezzlement. W. B., who was tried and acquitted of similar charges, was forced to borrow heavily from his brother to cover Coney's losses and ultimately forfeited all his holdings, including his bank at Texline and six thousand acres of land in Dallam and Hartley counties, to him. He also gave up his interest in Bankers' Trust. Perhaps because of W. B.'s financial crisis, the company failed to attract major investments and apparently was liquidated.

W. B.'s financial relationship with his brother had always been strained. In 1898 W. B. had purchased land in Sherman County in the upper Texas Panhandle with a $30,000 loan from the Colonel. Seven years later, with $25,000 of the loan unpaid, he attempted unsuccessfully to get his brother to accept a $15,000 payoff. To son George, Colonel Slaughter wrote of his brother, "[Bill] has a lot of gall, hasn't he?" However, in spite of W. B.'s mishandling of Bankers' Trust, the Colonel went to the rescue of his brother in another way. In September 1916 he employed W. B. to succeed Jack Alley (who leased the remnant of Slaughter's Running Water Ranch) as manager of the Long S Ranch. Unfortunately, less than a week after Colonel Slaughter's death on January 25, 1919, W. B. attempted to sell Bob Slaughter's newly acquired Western S Ranch, which lay on the Rio Grande in Hudspeth County, to "an unknown Mexican company." When Bob happened to learn about the fraudulent negotiations, he confronted and fired his uncle on February 8, 1919. "[W. B.] is a thief," reported Bob to his brother Dick, "and he admits it before C. C. [Jr.] and me." Two years later W. B. filed a three-million-dollar slander suit against his nephews, but there is no evidence that he ever collected anything.[12]

The unhappy experience with W. B. Slaughter and Bankers' Trust Company ended Colonel Slaughter's business ventures. No longer able to travel extensively, he was content to live out his days peacefully. He continued to visit the refurbished Long S Ranch annually, usually spending the summer at Soash. He often had his chauffeur drive to a herd of cattle, honk the auto's horn, and silently watch the cattle as they crowded around the car. "As they gazed wonderingly at Colonel Slaughter," recorded a Dallas observer, "he would beam back delighted just to feast his eyes on them."

Even with his declining health, Slaughter continued to enjoy excellent profits from his investments, particularly from the old Long S.

Restocked in 1913, the ranch had 8,327 head of cattle on April 10, 1914, including 1,413 newly purchased two-year-old steers. In 1915 the ranch returned a net profit of $106,186.84, or 23 percent on the $451,139.00 investment.

Meanwhile, Slaughter's children, who had assumed complete ownership of the Lazy S in 1911, initially enjoyed handsome profits from that enterprise. For each of the ten stockholders (including Mrs. C. C. Slaughter), its dividend increased from a modest five hundred dollars in 1911 to ten thousand dollars in 1913. In midsummer of 1915, however, the Slaughter family suffered a reversal from which there was no recovery. When George Slaughter died, no one could fill his place. His hard work and devotion to family business had resulted in profitable returns from the ranches during the twenty-five years he had managed the Running Water and Lazy S. Although the company ranch ran smoothly for a few months under Bob Slaughter's direction, profits soon sagged and expenses mounted.

In addition, disastrous weather problems soon plunged the once smoothly running Lazy S into turmoil. The parching drought of 1917, followed by a tragic snowstorm and blizzard in January, reminiscent of those of the 1880s, took a heavy toll of cattle. By the end of 1920, the Lazy S's indebtedness had increased to $270,000; simultaneously, annual cattle sales had dropped to only $20,000.[13]

Colonel Slaughter was spared the agony of witnessing the final demise of his empire. On January 25, 1919, two weeks before his eighty-second birthday, the old cattleman died. Newspapers across the state lauded his long, productive life, especially noting his great wealth, his generous philanthropy, and his "most sensational act"—the purchase of Sir Bredwell. J. B. Cranfill in a special *Baptist Standard* editorial described him as "a man of dauntless courage" who "blazed the way for all the great [Baptist] achievements that we have known through the past quarter of a century." The *Cattleman*, official organ of the Texas and Southwestern Cattle Raisers Association, which Slaughter had helped found, recorded that "as a stockman, merchant, and banker, he was most successful and by his honest methods and square dealing amassed a great fortune." The *Dallas Times-Herald* recalled his humble start when he bought half-interest in his father's cattle herd with money he earned "peddling goods." From that venture in 1854 until his death in 1919, C. C. Slaughter rode thousands of miles along dusty cattle trails, negotiated shrewdly in cattle markets throughout the East and Midwest, and from behind his banker's desk made advantageous deals with fellow cattlemen that, altogether, enabled him to accumulate a fortune that on March 31, 1919, was estimated to be $3,208,248.94. That figure did not include the Lazy S Ranch, which Slaughter had given to his children in 1911. Its value was estimated in 1918 to be $928,000.

Funeral services for Christopher Columbus Slaughter were held on Sunday afternoon, January 26, at 3506 Worth Street, his home for forty-five years. In the absence of his pastor, George W. Truett, who was in Europe, longtime friend and associate J. B. Cranfill delivered the sermon. In his laudatory remarks, Cranfill dwelt primarily on the deceased's philanthropy to Baptist benevolences and to Baylor Hospital. He said that Slaughter had built his own monuments and that his name would forever be enshrined in the great institutions he loved. Cranfill concluded by pointing out that his longtime friend had tried to do the best that he could for his family, subtly implying that this was his only area of failure. Slaughter had given his children every opportunity for intellectual and spiritual advancement that a loving father's hand could provide. The children knew, Cranfill said, that the "glory of his life and his home will be in their hearts as an incense through all the after years." [14]

Unfortunately, within two years, "the glory of his life"—sixty-five years of building a vast West Texas empire—was undone by Slaughter's children. Although he willed that his estate be divided equally among his wife and nine children (George Slaughter's widow, Allie, was to receive his share), Slaughter, fearful that there would be dissension over the will, had stipulated that should his wife, Carrie Averill Slaughter, or a group of the children by either of his marriages contest the will, the entire fortune would pass to the others. His codicil was appropriate. For many years the children had divided during quarrels into two groups, the older (George, Bob, Minnie, Dick, and Dela) against the younger (C. C., Jr., Alexander, Carrie, and Nelle). Unable to agree on any joint arrangement for operation of the estate, the heirs were forced to effect complicated divisions of the property. As a result all the land was appraised and divided into ten tracts of equal value. Then on March 15, 1920, the family drew capsules from a hat, each containing brief descriptions of land parcels. In such a manner, the old Long S, the remnant of the Running Water, and W. B. Slaughter's former property were methodically divided into small tracts. The

Dallas property, notes receivable, stocks and bonds, furniture, personal effects, livestock, and $174,000 in cash were divided similarly.

Even Slaughter's "insurance policy," the 246,000-acre Lazy S Ranch, which he had proclaimed to be "indivisible," and the Slaughter Hereford Home near Roswell were divided. On August 20, 1920, because "of the dissension and dissatisfied stockholders," nine Slaughter heirs petitioned the directors of C. C. Slaughter Cattle Company for division. As a result, on April 11, 1921, it too was equally partitioned among the ten shareholders. By August 1921 the Slaughter cattle empire had vanished, and in its stead ten small ranches had supplanted a range that once was the "kingdom" of the famous Sir Bredwell.

The breakup of the Slaughter empire, however, did no financial harm to some Slaughter heirs. For those fortunate enough to inherit land in Cochran and Hockley counties, vast riches awaited. On April 8, 1937, on Bob Slaughter's tract of the old Lazy S, five miles south of Sundown, a Texaco oil well completion signaled the beginning of the great Slaughter oil field. With a production of 511 barrels a day, the discovery well created a boom, and within four years the field had 52,000 acres of proven production with 849 wells. By the end of 1975 total production had reached 642,687,368 barrels, or an approximate income to the landowners of twenty million dollars per year.[15]

Unfortunately, the dissolution of the vast ranching domain deprived Slaughter of the significant place in history he deserved. No longer did his far-flung cattle empire stand as a visible embodiment of his wealth and power, and the greatness of his accomplishments was forgotten as rapidly as his legacy was carved into hundreds of cotton and small grain farms. Furthermore, family disharmony, which continued beyond his own children's generation, prevented any united effort to memorialize his life. Actually, no effort on their part was necessary for, as J. B. Cranfill had told the mourners gathered at his funeral, Slaughter had "built his own monuments"—Baylor University and seven other Texas Baptist colleges, as a tribute to his appreciation of Christian education; Baylor Medical Center in Dallas, in 1979 a $100,000,000 complex, as an evidence of his humanitarianism; and a thriving cattle industry in West Texas, as testimony of his faith in the importance of land and cattle.

The product of an era that produced many "cattle kings,"[16] real and fictitious, Christopher Columbus Slaughter succeeded in earning his title. He was indeed a self-made man, driven from an early age by a competitive spirit born and bred on the Texas frontier. He was an excellent judge of beef cattle, a trait which gave him distinct advantages in buying or selling at markets. He had a good business mind, which probably prompted him to develop strong banking ties early in his career. During the formative years of the West Texas cattle business, land was cheap, labor was plentiful, but interest rates were always high. With the ability to borrow adequate capital with little or no interest, Slaughter was able to survive the inevitable West Texas droughts and cattle depressions.

During the development of his empire, Slaughter exploited both his family and business associates. He dominated the lives of his children, using his sons in all phases of his business. Even when he loaned them money, he did so at interest. Likewise, he often enlarged his cattle herds at the expense of an unfortunate West Texas cattleman. Slaughter's loans were always made with tight contracts; a debtor's default usually meant a sizable gain for Slaughter. However, he was not dishonest. Like many other turn-of-the-century philanthropists, he applied religion to his business. "He was absolutely just and straight in his dealings with friend and foe alike," said Jack Alley. "He acquired his property through shrewdness and foresight."

As an individual he was one of the major cattlemen of America. His landholdings compared favorably to those of California butcher and stock raiser Henry Miller, who controlled one million acres in five western states. Slaughter's wealth exceeded by $3,500,000 that of one of Montana's biggest cattle raisers, Pierre Wibaux. The size of Slaughter's herds never matched the reported 125,000 head owned by Washington stockman Ben Snipes. Snipes, however, went bankrupt during the Panic of 1893. Similarly, although Slaughter's land and cattle holdings were smaller than many of the investor-owned ranching companies of the Great Plains, his empire outlasted most.

Many of the nation's cattle barons were Texans. Among their number, Slaughter compared favorably to those whose biographies have been written. At his death in 1885, South Texas rancher Richard King, who established the famous King Ranch, owned 614,140 acres and 40,000 cattle, holdings of a similar size to Slaughter's. A. H. ("Shanghai") Pierce, another well-known and legendary South Texas stockman, was worth less than half the Slaughter fortune at his death in 1900. The colorful Charles Goodnight, whose name is nationally famous, repeatedly lost money in poor investments, never matched Slaughter's wealth, and at his death in 1929 was broke.[17]

Interestingly, Slaughter's career, except for politics, closely paralleled that of Texas entrepreneur George Washington Littlefield. Like "Colonel" Slaughter, "Major" Littlefield made a fortune after the Civil War by driving cattle to Kansas. In 1877, while Slaughter was establishing the Long S Ranch in West Texas, Littlefield was founding his LIT Ranch on free range along the Canadian River in the Texas Panhandle. Littlefield in 1890 founded the American National Bank in Austin, which coincidentally bore the same name as the bank Slaughter had established in Dallas six years before. In 1882 Littlefield purchased an irrigated farm in the Pecos River valley near Roswell, New Mexico, eighteen years before Slaughter bought his Hereford Home. In 1901 Littlefield bought the XIT's 300,000-acre Yellow House Ranch in Hockley and Lamb counties, which lay adjacent to Slaughter's Lazy S Ranch, and thereafter for the life of the two cattlemen, these ranches shared a common fence. And at the time of Slaughter's death in 1919, Littlefield's holdings and total wealth were similar to that of his neighbor.

In *The Cattle Kings*, historian Lewis Atherton wrote, "The skill with which men like Goodnight, Iliff, Kohrs, Littlefield, Story, and a host of others combined the commonly recognized factors of production—land, labor and capital—certainly substantiates the argument of those economists who insist on recognizing a fourth factor, namely, entrepreneurship." Like Littlefield and the others named by Atherton, C. C. Slaughter was a true entrepreneur. He exhibited entrepreneurial flexibility by adapting from trail driving to cattle raising to improved breeding. He demonstrated a willingness to work at regional and national levels to improve the cattle industry as a whole, thereby aiding his own business. Always an optimist, he possessed the daring of a gambler as he risked cattle herds on a war-ravaged frontier, as he moved forty-two thousand dollars in an open wagon across sixty miles of dangerous roads to open a bank, and as he bought half a county of West Texas land considered to be worthless. Slaughter gambled, and his risks paid off handsomely. Thus, he emerged as a cattle king able to survive the transition from the open range to modern cattle ranching. For this kind of success, Atherton perhaps best defined the formula:

"By luck alone, one might profit greatly from a single venture of short duration, but only an entrepreneur possessed of daring, flexibility, curiosity, and a willingness to change procedures, could hope to retain his place among the cattle kings for any extended period of time." [18] Christopher Columbus Slaughter, virtually unknown to Atherton, could have served as the historian's best model.

Appendix: The
C. C. Slaughter Family

Christopher Columbus Slaughter, 1837–1919, m. 1861 Cynthia Ann Jowell, 1844–1876

George Morgan, 1862–1915, m. Alice Louise Donohoo
    Minnie Magdalene   Jo Dick
    George Morgan, Jr.   Eloise [Hill]

Minnie, 1864–1955, m. George T. Veal

Dela, 1866–1956, m. Gilbert Greer Wright
    Gilbert Greer, Jr.   Jowell Slaughter
    Florence Roberta [Reeves]   Stuart Phillips
    Ed Dela [Catto]

Eugene, 1868–1870

Robert Lee, 1870–1938, m. Florence Harris, m. Belle
    Robert Lee, Jr.

Edgar Dick, 1873–1935, m. Carrie Ligon Graham, m. Sally Tibbs Milleken
    Edgar Dick, Jr.

m. 1877 Carrie Averill, 1852–1928

C. C., Jr., 1879–1940, m. Elma Letcher
    Anella [Bauer]

Walter Webb, 1880–1881

Alexander Averill, 1881–1931, m. Blanche Fallon, m. Dorothy Gray

Hattie Louise [Browning]

Carrie Rebecca, 1883–1958, m. John Henry Dean
John Henry, Jr.

Nelle Louise, 1892–1964, m. Ira Pleasant Deloache
Averill
Nelle Jordan [Davidson]
James Ira

Notes

1. Frontier Beginnings

1. See Don W. Slaughter, "Anyone Interested?" (typescript), Slaughter Family Reference File, Southwest Collection, Texas Tech University, Lubbock (hereafter cited as Slaughter File). For many years genealogists linked the Slaughters of Texas to a prominent Virginia family centered in Culpepper County. This family has been traced to 1619 or 1620, when John Slaughter received land grants in Rappahannock County, Virginia, and settled there. "Known Ancestors of Anella Slaughter Bauer of Texas" (typescript), in possession of Mrs. Richard Bauer, Dallas, Texas. See also Raleigh Travers Green, *Genealogical and Historical Notes on Culpepper County, Virginia, Embracing a Revised and Enlarged Edition of Dr. Philip Slaughter's History of St. Mark's Parish* (Baltimore: Regional Publishing, 1964), pp. 28, 29.

A recent genealogical study by John Frederick Dorman discounts any connection between the Culpepper County Slaughters and the Texas family. John Frederick Dorman to Elmer Slaughter, Sept. 15, 1970 (Xerox), Elmer Slaughter, "Slaughter Family History" (typescript), Slaughter File.

2. Slaughter, "Anyone Interested?" p. 4; James Cox, ed., *The Cattle Industry and the Cattlemen of Texas and Adjacent Territory* (St. Louis: Woodward and Tiernan, 1895), p. 303; Slaughter, "Slaughter Family History." The Cox account is based on an interview in 1894 with George Webb Slaughter, father of C. C., shortly before his death and is the most complete firsthand account of his experiences.

3. Allen Erwin, *The Southwest of John H. Slaughter* (Glendale, Calif.: Arthur H. Clark, 1965), p. 37 n.; David M. Vigness, *The Revolutionary Decades* (Austin: Steck-Vaughn, 1965), p. 109; William Kennedy, *Texas: The Rise, Progress, and Prospects of the Republic of Texas* (1841; rpt. Fort Worth: Molyneaux Craftsmen, 1925), p. 139; *Abstract of Valid Land Claims Compiled from the Records of the General*

Land Office and Court of Claims of the State of Texas (Austin: John Marshall, 1859), p. 476; Cox, *Cattle Industry*, pp. 303–304; *An Abstract of the Original Title of Record in the General Land Office, Houston, 1838* (rpt. Austin: Pemberton Press, 1964), pp. 149–150; George W. Smyth, "The Autobiography of George W. Smyth," *Southwestern Historical Quarterly*, 36 (Jan. 1933), 210; Alexander Horton, "Life of Alexander Horton and Early Settlement of San Augustine County," *Quarterly of the Texas State Historical Association*, 14 (Apr. 1911), 308–309; R. B. Blake, *Historic Nacogdoches* (Nacogdoches: Nacogdoches Historical Society, 1939), pp. 10–11; Llerena Friend, *Sam Houston: The Great Designer* (Austin: University of Texas Press, 1954), p. 54.

4. Cox, *Cattle Industry*, p. 304; John Henry Brown, *History of Texas* (2 vols.; St. Louis: L. E. Daniell, 1892), I, 408; "Lieutenant George Webb Slaughter" (typescript), Daughters of the Republic of Texas Library, San Antonio, Texas; John Henry Brown, *Indian Wars and Pioneers of Texas* (Austin: L. E. Daniell, n.d.), painting of Slaughter following p. 668; Marion Day Mullins, *The First Census of Texas, 1829–1836* (Washington, D.C.: National Genealogical Society, 1959), p. 39; *Prose and Poetry of the Livestock Industry of the United States* (Kansas City: National Livestock Association, 1904), p. 521; J. C. Koen, "George Webb Slaughter," *West Texas Historical Association Year Book*, 28 (1952), 109.

5. John H. Reagan, "The Expulsion of the Cherokees from East Texas," *Quarterly of the Texas State Historical Association*, 1 (July 1897), 44–46; Dorman H. Winfrey and James M. Day, eds., *Texas Indian Papers* (4 vols.; Austin: Texas State Library, 1959–1961), I, 77; United States Seventh Census (1850), Population, Sabine County, Texas, National Archives, Washington, D.C. (Microcopy No. M-432, Roll 914). Nancy, the second child, was born in 1840; George Webb, Jr., in 1843; Peter E. in 1844; and John B. in 1848.

6. United States Seventh Census (1850), Agriculture, Sabine County, Texas, Texas State Library, Austin, Texas (Microcopy Roll 3); Cox, *Cattle Industry*, p. 304; Walter Prescott Webb, H. Bailey Carroll, and Eldon Stephen Branda, eds., *The Handbook of Texas* (3 vols.; Austin: Texas State Historical Association, 1952, 1976), II, 618; Dorman to Elmer Slaughter, Apr. 25, 1971, Slaughter File; J. Marvin Hunter, ed., *The Trail Drivers of Texas* (2d ed. rev.; Nashville: Cokesbury Press, 1925), p. 865. Another son, William Baxter, was born in Freestone County in 1852.

7. Cox, *Cattle Industry*, p. 332; "Colonel C. C. Slaughter," *Frontier Times*, 8 (July 1931), 433–437; *Prose and Poetry*, p. 521; J. Frank Dobie, *The Longhorns* (rpt. Boston: Little, Brown, 1941), p. 48.

8. *Memorial and Biographical History of Navarro, Henderson, Anderson, Limestone, Freestone, and Leon Counties, Texas* (Chicago: Lewis, 1893), p. 402; *Prose and Poetry*, pp. 521–522; "Early Trade and Travel Routes," in William C. Pool, *A Historical Atlas of Texas* (Austin: Encino Press, 1975), pp. 106–107. The Slaughters apparently followed the military roads leading from Fort Houston in Anderson County to Fort Graham and other points farther west.

9. Cox, *Cattle Industry*, p. 333; United States Eighth Census (1860), Population, Palo Pinto County, Texas, National Archives (Microcopy No. M-432, Roll 913). By 1857 the family included C. C., George, Jr., Peter, John, Wil-

liam B., and Francis. After the move to Palo Pinto, two daughters, Mary and Sarah Jane, were born in 1858 and 1860 respectively.

10. J. Evetts Haley, *Charles Goodnight: Cowman and Plainsman* (Norman: University of Oklahoma Press, 1949), p. 33; Robert S. Neighbors to contractors Preston Webb and Pleasant Webb, June 15, 1857, and Quarterly Reports, U.S. Bureau of Indian Affairs, Letters Received, Texas Agency, 1847–1859, National Archives (Microcopy No. 234, Roll 860).

11. Ernest Wallace, *Texas in Turmoil* (Austin: Steck-Vaughn, 1965), p. 21; Rupert N. Richardson, *The Comanche Barrier to South Plains Settlement* (Glendale, Calif.: Arthur H. Clark, 1933), pp. 251–252; Carrie J. Crouch, *A History of Young County* (Austin: Texas State Historical Association, 1956), p. 22; Cox, *Cattle Industry*, p. 332; Haley, *Charles Goodnight*, p. 26; J. J. Sturm to S. P. Ross, Dec. 30, 1858, Jan. 15, 1859, in *Report of the Secretary of the Interior*, Sen. Exec. Doc. No. 2, 36th Cong., 1st sess., 1860, p. 600; Kenneth Neighbours, *Robert Simpson Neighbors and the Texas Frontier* (Waco: Texian Press, 1975), p. 224.

12. Cox, *Cattle Industry*, p. 332; Winfrey and Day, eds., *Texas Indian Papers*, III, 312–313; Citizens to Neighbors, Apr. 25, 1859, Ross to Neighbors, May 12, 1859, Neighbors to A. B. Greenwood, July 24, 1859, *Report . . . Interior*, 1860, pp. 639, 641–642, 687; W. J. Hughes, *Rebellious Ranger* (Norman: University of Oklahoma Press, 1964), p. 154; Neighbours, *Neighbors*, pp. 236, 246, 271–273; Kenneth Neighbours, *Indian Exodus: Texas Indian Affairs* (Quanah, Tex.: Nortex Offset, 1973), p. 136; Wallace, *Texas in Turmoil*, p. 26.

13. Richardson, *Comanche Barrier*, p. 153; Friend, *Sam Houston*, p. 325; Haley, *Charles Goodnight*, p. 48; Wallace, *Texas in Turmoil*, p. 27; Winfrey and Day, eds., *Texas Indian Papers*, IV, 1–2; Amelia W. Williams and Eugene C. Barker, eds., *The Writings of Sam Houston, 1813–1863* (8 vols.; Austin: University of Texas Press, 1938–1943), VII, 507; United States Eighth Census (1860), Agriculture, Palo Pinto County, Texas, Texas State Library (Microcopy No. 2).

14. James H. Baker, "Diary of J. H. Baker, 1858–1918" (typescript), pp. 112, 141, Archives Division, Texas State Library; Koen, "George Webb Slaughter," p. 110; Zane Allen Mason, *Frontiersmen of the Faith* (San Antonio: Naylor, 1970), p. 87; W. C. Holden to David Murrah, Mar. 2, 1970, interview; Crouch, *History of Young County*, p. 170.

15. United States Eighth Census (1860), Population, Palo Pinto County; Haley, *Charles Goodnight*, p. 18; Crouch, *History of Young County*, pp. 91, 134; Baker, "Diary," pp. 144, 146.

16. Ranger Muster Rolls Index, Archives Division, Texas State Library; Muster Roll, Dec. 5, 1860, C. C. Slaughter Papers, Southwest Collection, Texas Tech University (hereafter cited as CCS); Baker, "Diary," p. 33; Carl Coke Rister, *Fort Griffin on the Texas Frontier* (Norman: University of Oklahoma Press, 1956), p. 29; Haley, *Charles Goodnight*, p. 53; John M. Elkins, *Indian Fighting on the Texas Frontier* (n.p., 1929), p. 35; Clyde L. Jackson and Grace Jackson, *Quanah Parker, Last Chief of the Comanches* (New York: Exposition Press, 1963), p. 39.

For many years Ross believed that he had killed Peta Nocona, father of Quanah Parker. However, Haley indicates that the chief killed No-bah and that Nocona died many years later while hunting plums along the Canadian River.

For varying accounts of Nocona's death, see Haley, *Charles Goodnight*, p. 57, and Rupert N. Richardson, ed., "The Death of Nocona and the Recovery of Cynthia Ann Parker," *Southwestern Historical Quarterly*, 46 (July 1942), 15–21. See also Ross' narrative of the expedition in James T. DeShields, *Cynthia Ann Parker* (St. Louis: by the author, 1886), pp. 61–66; J. W. Wilbarger, *Indian Depredations in Texas* (Austin: Hutchings, 1889), p. 336; E. E. White, *Experiences of a Special Agent* (Norman: University of Oklahoma, 1965), pp. 263–272.

17. Haley, *Charles Goodnight*, pp. 55, 61; Baker, "Diary," p. 210; Wilbarger, *Indian Depredations*, p. 338; W. C. Cochran, "Story of Early Day Indian Troubles and Cattle Business of Palo Pinto and Adjoining Counties" (typescript), p. 11, Archives, University of Texas at Austin; *Dallas Herald*, Jan. 2, 1861.

18. Cox, *Cattle Industry*, pp. 304, 322; Baker, "Diary," pp. 190, 243; Ranger Muster Rolls Index, Archives Division, Texas State Library. After the war Slaughter filed a claim for $431.71 for unpaid service in 1861. Of this amount $297.66 was for his three-month service as lieutenant of the Palo Pinto Ranger Company. Winfrey and Day, eds. *Texas Indian Papers*, IV, 118–119. See also Confederate Audited Military Claims, 1862–1865, No. 1020, Comptroller's Records, Archives Division, Texas State Library.

19. Williams and Barker, eds., *Writings of Sam Houston*, VII, 386, 503, 507; E. W. Winkler, ed., *Journal of the Secession Convention of Texas. 1861* (Austin: Texas State Library, 1912), pp. 384–385; Ranger Muster Roll Index, Archives Division, Texas State Library. The only source documenting Slaughter's presence at Camp Cooper, a reference in Confederate Veterans Reunion Scrapbook, CCS, dated 1901, reads: "He [Slaughter] was commissioned an officer at the outbreak of the war on the frontier and was serving on the state border when he and his command was mustered into the Confederate service at Camp Griffin." Since Fort Griffin was not established until 1867, the writer's (and probably Slaughter's) reference must have been to nearby Camp Cooper.

20. H. P. N. Gammel, comp., *The Laws of Texas* (10 vols.; Austin: Gammel, 1898), V, 346; Wallace, *Texas in Turmoil*, p. 235; *Prose and Poetry*, p. 523; Winfrey and Day, eds., *Texas Indian Papers*, IV, 67–68.

21. Baker, "Diary," pp. 288–289.

22. George A. Wallis, *Cattle Kings of the Staked Plains* (Denver: Sage, 1964), p. 65; Gammel, comp., *Laws of Texas*, V, 453; William C. Pool, ed., "Westward I Go Free: The Memoirs of William E. Cureton, Texas Frontiersman," *Southwestern Historical Quarterly*, 81 (Oct. 1977), 170. Only the last source indicates that Slaughter served in the Frontier Regiment in 1862. William E. Cureton, J. J. Cureton's son, wrote that "Goodnight, [C. C.] Slaughter, and Sanger again cast their fortunes with him [J. J. Cureton]; were first stationed at Old Fort Belknap on the upper Brazos in Young County."

23. Wilbarger, *Indian Depredations*, pp. 510–511; Baker, "Diary," pp. 318, 334–335; Gammel, comp., *Laws of Texas*, V, 677–679; Ranger Muster Roll, 1864, Adjutant General's Office Records, Austin, Texas; Kenneth Neighbours, "Elm Creek Raid in Young County, 1864," *West Texas Historical Association Year Book*, 40 (1964), 89. One severe raid did occur in October 1864. Two hundred Comanches and Kiowas attacked "Fort" Murrah, a Confederate outpost near Fort

Belknap, killing five troopers. Then the Indians struck the nearby Elm Creek settlement, taking seven lives and capturing seven women and children.

24. Dayton Kelley, "The Tonkawas," in *Indian Wars of Texas* (Waco: Texian Press, 1971), p. 163; Hunter, *Trail Drivers of Texas*, p. 865.

25. Wallace, *Texas in Turmoil*, p. 244; Haley, *Charles Goodnight*, pp. 103–104; Cox, *Cattle Industry*, pp. 332–333; *Prose and Poetry*, p. 61. Goodnight's recollections of the shooting vary. In an early account, he vividly described the accident, but in later memoirs he indicated that he left the group after two days on the trail, deciding that "after all it would be better to hunt a market for his cattle than a home for them." A Shackelford County settler at Fort Davis noted in his diary on March 4, 1866, that "parson Slaughter would not be up to preach because Lum [Slaughter] was wounded." Samuel P. Newcomb, Diary, 1865–1873 (typescript), Mar. 4, 1866, Archives, University of Texas at Austin.

26. C. C. Slaughter to W. H. Harrison, Mar. 17, 1886, interview (manuscript, microfilm), Bancroft Library, University of California at Berkeley.

2. Cattleman and Banker

1. Cochran, "Story of Early Day Indian Troubles," p. 39.

2. Cox, *Cattle Industry*, p. 305; United States Eighth Census (1860), Agriculture, Jack County, Texas, Texas State Library (Microcopy No. 8); United States Ninth Census (1870), Agriculture, Jack County, Texas, Texas State Library (Microcopy No. 28); Wallace, *Texas in Turmoil*, p. 243; *Texas Almanac and State Industrial Guide, 1972–1973* (Dallas: A. H. Belo, 1971), pp. 158–160; Wayne Gard, *The Chisholm Trail* (Norman: University of Oklahoma Press, 1954), pp. 29–39.

3. *Dallas Morning News*, Feb. 10, 1917; Hunter, *Trail Drivers of Texas*, p. 865; W. B. Slaughter, as quoted in Cora Melton Cross, "Stories of Old Trail Drives of Long Ago," *Semi-Weekly Farm News* (Dallas), July 24, 1936; Cora Melton Cross, "Up the Trail with Nine Million Longhorns," *Texas Monthly*, 5 (Feb. 1930), 143–144. The Slaughter trail drive to Jefferson is mentioned in several accounts and is the most repeated story in the Slaughter family annals. See also Cox, *Cattle Industry*, p. 333.

4. Slaughter to Harrison, Mar. 17, 1886, interview; Cox, *Cattle Industry*, pp. 305, 348; *Memorial and Biographical History of Dallas County, Texas* (Chicago: Lewis, 1892), p. 520; Cattle Record Book, 1870, pp. 102–116, Records, Palo Pinto County Courthouse, Palo Pinto, Texas; *Dallas Morning News*, Feb. 2, 1917; William M. Raine and Will C. Barnes, *Cattle* (Garden City, N.Y.: Doubleday, Doran, 1930), p. 74; Gard, *Chisholm Trail*, p. 55; Dee Brown, *Trail Driving Days* (New York: Charles Scribner's Sons, 1952), p. 8; Harry Sinclair Drago, *Great American Cattle Trails* (New York: Dodd, Mead, 1965), p. 100; W. B. Slaughter, as cited in Hunter, *Trail Drivers of Texas*, pp. 865–866. Although Bill Slaughter's account is comprehensive, his dating is apparently off by one year. For example, he indicated that Charlie Rivers' death occurred in 1872, but all other sources cite June 16, 1871.

5. Cross, "Stories of Old Trail Drives"; Cox, *Cattle Industry*, pp. 303, 305;

Hunter, *Trail Drivers of Texas*, pp. 69−70; Baker, "Diary," pp. 387, 398, 401; Ernest S. Osgood, *The Day of the Cattleman* (Minneapolis: University of Minnesota Press, 1929), p. 46; U.S. House, *Range and Ranch Cattle Traffic*, House Exec. Doc. No. 267, 48th Cong., 2d sess., 1885, p. 31; *Dallas Herald*, July 18, 1874; Cora Melton Cross, "William B. Slaughter, Trail Drive of 1866," *Frontier Times*, 6 (Aug. 1929), 466; Mary Whatley Dunbar, "Two Daughters of the Frontier," *Frontier Times*, 15 (Feb. 1938), 186; Bill of Sale, Mortgage of Personal Property Record Book, 1872, pp. 103−106, Palo Pinto County Courthouse.

6. Hunter, *Trail Drivers of Texas*, pp. 870, 919; Cox, *Cattle Industry*, p. 305; Winfrey and Day, eds., *Texas Indian Papers*, IV, 381; Ernest Wallace, ed., *Ranald S. Mackenzie's Official Correspondence Relating to Texas, 1871−1873* (Lubbock: West Texas Museum Association, 1967), pp. 24−25; Benjamin Capps, *The Warren Wagontrain Raid* (New York: Dial Press, 1974), pp. 47−53; Cattle Record Book, 1871, pp. 45−63, Mortgage of Personal Property Record Book, 1872, pp. 103−106, Deed Records, vol. D, p. 502, Palo Pinto County Courthouse.

7. Cox, *Cattle Industry*, pp. 305, 333; Cuthbert Powell, *Twenty Years of Kansas City's Livestock Trade and Traders* (Kansas City: Pearl, 1893), pp. 38−39; Gard, *Chisholm Trail*, pp. 222 n., 307; Rupert N. Richardson, "William S. Ikard and Hereford Raising in Texas," *West Texas Historical Association Year Book*, 25 (1949), 45−46; *Livestock World* (Chicago), June 23, 1902; Hunter, *Trail Drivers of Texas*, p. 388; Historical Society, "Scrapbook History of Mineral Wells and Palo Pinto County," Mineral Wells Municipal Library, Mineral Wells, Texas.

8. Cox, *Cattle Industry*, p. 383; *Prose and Poetry*, p. 383; Laura V. Hamner, "Life Began in the Seventies" (typescript, microfilm), p. 315, Southwest Collection, Texas Tech University; *Dallas Herald*, May 24, 1873; A. C. Greene, *Dallas: The Deciding Years* (Austin: Encino Press, 1973), pp. 23−24; Ruby Keith, "Early History of Dallas" (M.A. thesis, University of Texas, 1930), p. 126. The Houston and Texas Central Railway did extend its tracks to Denison, but the portion between Dallas and Denison was never of prime importance. Westward expansion of the Texas and Pacific beyond Dallas was delayed for three years by the Panic of 1873.

9. Historical Chart Depicting the Ancestry of the First National Bank in Dallas, in *Half a Century of Constructive Service* (n.p., 1939), n.p.; Gammel, comp., *Laws of Texas*, VII, 1436−1438; Joseph M. Grant and Lawrence L. Crum, *The Development of State-Chartered Banking in Texas* (Austin: University of Texas System, 1978), p. 28; W. E. McAnally to David Murrah, June 25, 1970, interview; *Prose and Poetry*, p. 383; W. E. H. [William E. Hughes] Gramp, *The Journal of a Grandfather* (St. Louis: by the author, 1912), p. 138; *Dallas Herald*, June 7, 1873.

10. *Directory of the City of Dallas for the Year 1875* (St. Louis: Democrat Litho and Print, n.d.), pp. 68−69; Cox, *Cattle Industry*, p. 303; *Dallas Herald*, Oct. 24, 1874, May 20, 1876, Jan. 27, 1877; R. G. Dun & Co. to A. M. Averill, Oct. 5, 1876, Carrie Averill Slaughter Papers, Southwest Collection, Texas Tech University (hereafter cited as CAS); John William Rogers, *The Lusty Texans of Dallas* (New York: E. P. Dutton, 1951), p. 105; United States Tenth Census (1880), Agriculture, Dallas County, Texas, Texas State Library (Microcopy No. 23).

11. George A. Wallis, *Cattle Kings of the Staked Plains* (Dallas: American Guild Press, 1957), p. 25; Carrie Averill to C. C. Slaughter, Aug. 8, Sept. 27, 1876, R. G. Dun & Co. to A. M. Averill, Oct. 5, 1876, C. C. Slaughter to A. M. Averill, Dec. 20, 1876, CAS; *Dallas Herald*, Jan. 27, 1877.

12. Cox, *Cattle Industry*, p. 334; Wallace, *Texas in Turmoil*, p. 260; Haley, *Charles Goodnight*, pp. 263, 267, 277, 301–302; "Ranching" (typescript, microfilm), p. 4, John L. McCarty Papers, Southwest Collection, Texas Tech University.

13. Rufus O'Keefe, *Cowboy Life* (San Antonio: Naylor, 1936), p. 106; *Texas Livestock Journal* (Fort Worth), Oct. 28, 1882; Carrie Averill to C. C. Slaughter, Aug. 8, 1876, CAS; Jack Alley, as told to Frank P. Hill, "Fifty-four Years of Pioneering on the Plains of Texas," *Lynn County News* (Tahoka), Apr. 28–Aug. 4, 1931 (Xerox), Jack Alley Reference File, Southwest Collection, Texas Tech University (hereafter cited as Alley, "Fifty-four Years of Pioneering"); Mrs. J. Lee Jones and O. W. Cline, "Frontier Days in Mitchell County and Colorado City," *West Texas Historical Association Year Book*, 16 (1940), 35; R. H. Looney, "A History of Colorado, Texas" (typescript), p. 14, Southwest Collection, Texas Tech University.

14. C. W. Foor to J. Evetts Haley, Sept. 23, 1927, interview (typescript), p. 4, in possession of J. Evetts Haley, Canyon, Texas; *Texas Livestock Journal*, Oct. 28, 1882; Alley, "Fifty-four Years of Pioneering"; O'Keefe, *Cowboy Life*, pp. 32–48; *Dallas Herald*, May 11, 1878; *Pleasanton Stock Journal*, as quoted in *Fort Worth Democrat*, July 31, 1875; Lewis Atherton, *The Cattle Kings* (Bloomington: Indiana University Press, 1961), p. 3; Richard H. Peterson, *The Bonanza Kings* (Lincoln: University of Nebraska Press, 1977), p. 3.

3. An Open Range Empire

1. Gilbert Webb, ed., *Four Score Years in Jack County* (n.p., n.d.), p. 25; Chester V. Kielman, "The Texas and Southwestern Cattle Raisers Association Minute Book," *Southwestern Historical Quarterly*, 71 (July 1967), 92 n., 93 n., 95; *Frontier Echo* (Jacksboro), Jan. 19, 1877; Cochran, "Story of Early Day Indian Troubles," p. 39; Crouch, *History of Young County*, p. 137; *Texas Almanac, 1966–1967*, pp. 131–132; Mary Whatley Clarke, *The Palo Pinto Story* (Fort Worth: Manney, 1956), p. 88; *Graham Leader*, Mar. 16, 1877; Minute Book, 1877–1892, Cattle Raisers Association of Northwestern Texas, pp. 12, 14, Records, Texas and Southwestern Cattle Raisers Association, Archives, University of Texas at Austin (hereafter cited as Minute Book, Cattle Raisers Association); *Fort Worth Gazette*, Mar. 7, 1883.

2. Crouch, *History of Young County*, p. 141; Jack Allison Rickard, "The Ranch Industry of the Texas South Plains" (M.A. thesis, University of Texas, 1927), p. 180; Hunter, *Trail Drivers of Texas*, p. 901; Alley, "Fifty-four Years of Pioneering"; Foor to Haley, Sept. 23, 1927, interview.

3. Revised Map of the State of Texas (n.p.: Houston and Texas Central Railroad, 1876), Southwest Collection, Texas Tech University. While walking his railroad survey in 1853, Captain John Pope passed within a few miles of Slaugh-

ter's first headquarters on the Colorado. See U.S. Pacific Rail Road Exploration and Survey Geological Map, U.S. War Department, *Reports of Explorations and Surveys, 1853—54*, vol. 2, Sen. Exec. Doc. No. 78, 33d Cong., 2d sess., 1854, Attachment.

4. Wynonna Jones, "History of Colonel C. C. Slaughter and His Lazy S Ranch" (typescript), Southwest Collection, Texas Tech University; Alley, "Fifty-four Years of Pioneering"; *Fort Griffin Echo*, Dec. 20, 1879; James L. Rock and W. I. Smith, *Southern and Western Texas Guide for 1878* (St. Louis: A. H. Granger, 1878), p. 240 and accompanying map; *Prose and Poetry*, p. 383; Cox, *Cattle Industry*, p. 303; Foor to Haley, Sept. 23, 1927, interview.

5. *Texas Livestock Journal*, Oct. 28, 1882, Feb. 17, 1883; O'Keefe, *Cowboy Life*, pp. 46—47, 51; unidentified newspaper clipping, Ranching File, McCarty Papers; Leona Marguerite Gelin, "Organization and Development of Dawson County to 1917" (M.A. thesis, Texas Technological College, 1937), p. 39; *Dallas Morning News*, Nov. 7, 1885; Alley, "Fifty-four Years of Pioneering"; Eugene H. Price, *Open Range Ranching on the South Plains in the 1890's* (Clarendon, Tex.: Clarendon Press, 1967), map (inside file pocket). Price's sketch map of the cow outfits on the South Plains was drawn from memory in 1936.

6. "Panhandle Plains Chronology" (typescript), McCarty Papers; W. Turrentine Jackson, *The Enterprising Scot* (Edinburgh: Edinburgh University Press, 1968), pp. 74—78; W. C. Holden, *The Espuela Land and Cattle Company* (Austin: Texas State Historical Association, 1970), pp. 42—43; Lester Fields Sheffy, *The Francklyn Land and Cattle Company* (Austin: University of Texas Press, 1963), pp. 1—140; "The Two-Buckle Ranch" (typescript), p. 3, Southwest Collection, Texas Tech University; William M. Pearce, *The Matador Land and Cattle Company* (Norman: University of Oklahoma Press, 1964), pp. 3—226; J. Fred Rippy, "British Investments in Texas Land and Livestock," *Southwestern Historical Quarterly*, 58 (Jan. 1955), 338; Al Hill, "Bob Slaughter's Half-Million Dollar Ride," *Lubbock News*, Jan. 20, 1932, Bob Slaughter Reference File, Southwest Collection, Texas Tech University; Curtis Bishop, "Race for a Half-Million," *True West*, 2 (Aug.—Sept. 1954), 22—23; R. L. Slaughter, "How the Big Springs Ranch Was Saved," in *The Big Springs Country of Texas*, pamphlet (1909), pp. 23—27, W. P. Soash Papers, Southwest Collection, Texas Tech University; Jess Slaughter to David Murrah, Dec. 10, 1976, interview.

7. Slaughter to Harrison, Mar. 17, 1886, interview; Cox, *Cattle Industry*, p. 333; *Dallas Morning News*, Feb. 10, 1917; *Livestock World*, June 23, 1902; Foor to Haley, Sept. 23, 1927, interview; *Dallas Morning News*, Nov. 7, 1885, Feb. 10, 1917; *Texas Livestock Journal*, Jan. 13, 1883, Mar. 7, 1885, Feb. 25, 1888; Hunter, *Trail Drivers of Texas*, p. 346; *Fort Griffin Echo*, Jan. 21, 1880. The Brazos and Colorado Cattlemen's Association became the South Panhandle Cattlemen's Association in 1888 and later merged with the Northwest Texas Cattle Raisers Association.

8. Bob Slaughter, as quoted in Jones, "C. C. Slaughter"; *Texas Livestock Journal*, Sept. 30, 1882; J. T. Small, *Daugherty Land and Cattle Company*, pamphlet (1891), W. B. Munson Papers, Archives, Panhandle-Plains Museum, West Texas State University, Canyon, Texas; *Dallas Morning News*, Feb. 10, 1917; Mary

Kiser Pinkerton, "The Running Water Community," *Hale County History*, 3 (May 1973), 7; Mary L. Cox, *History of Hale County, Texas* (Plainview: Mary L. Cox, 1937), p. 8; Cox, *Cattle Industry*, p. 498; O'Keefe, *Cowboy Life*, p. 32.

9. Hunter, *Trail Drivers of Texas*, p. 872; Edward Everett Dale, "Ranching on the Cheyenne-Arapaho Reservation, 1880–1885," *Chronicles of Oklahoma*, 6 (Mar. 1928), 35; Edward Everett Dale, "Ranching on the Cheyenne-Arapaho Reservation," *Cattleman*, 15 (Dec. 1928), 22–23; Donald J. Berthrong, "Cattlemen on the Cheyenne-Arapaho Reservation, 1883–1885," *Arizona and the West*, 13 (Spring 1971), 8–11; Minute Book, 1885, Records, Hunter and Evans Land and Cattle Company, Southwest Collection, Texas Tech University; *Texas Livestock Journal*, April 5–19, 26, 1884. Neither of the last two sources indicate how much Slaughter received for the cattle. Market prices in April 1884 averaged six cents a pound for Texas beef. If Slaughter's cattle averaged six hundred pounds per head, his gross price would have been $268,000.

10. O'Keefe, *Cowboy Life*, p. 64; Jimmy M. Skaggs, "Cattle Trails in Oklahoma," in Jimmy M. Skaggs, ed., *Ranch and Range in Oklahoma* (Oklahoma City: Oklahoma Historical Society, 1978), p. 14; *Fort Griffin Echo*, Feb. 28, Mar. 13, 1880, Mar. 19, 1881; Minute Book, Cattle Raisers Association, pp. 15–16, 21, 44, 56, 68–69; *Fort Worth Gazette*, Mar. 7, 1883; *Texas Livestock Journal*, Mar. 15, 1884.

11. Minute Book, Cattle Raisers Association, p. 91; Cox, *Cattle Industry*, p. 220; *Texas Livestock Journal*, Mar. 14, 1885; Slaughter to Harrison, Mar. 17, 1886, interview; *Dallas Morning News*, Mar. 11, 1886; *Fort Worth Gazette*, Mar. 10, 1887; Alley, "Fifty-four Years of Pioneering."

12. *Texas Livestock Journal*, Nov. 28, 1882; *Dallas City and County Directory, 1881–1882* (Dallas: Carter and Gibon, 1881), p. 85; *Morrison and Fourney's General Directory of the City of Dallas, 1884–1885* (Galveston: Clarke and Courts, 1884), p. 49. Subsequent mergers created the American Exchange National Bank. See Henry Camp Harris, Sr., *Dallas: Acorn Planters of Yesteryear, 1862–1964* (n.p., n.d.), p. 10, and James Howard, *Big D Is for Dallas* (Austin: Edwards Brothers, 1957), p. 52.

4. Survival of the Fittest

1. Cox, *Cattle Industry*, p. 196; James S. Brisbin, *The Beef Bonanza, or How to Get Rich on the Plains* (Philadelphia: J. B. Lippincott, 1882), pp. 69–70; Agnes Wright Spring, "A Genius for Handling Cattle: John W. Iliff," in Maurice Frink, W. Turrentine Jackson, and Agnes Wright Spring, *When Grass Was King* (Boulder: University of Colorado Press, 1956), p. 335; Atherton, *Cattle Kings*, p. 208; One contributor to Brisbin's book estimated that, utilizing an initial $7,875 investment, a person could within eleven years become worth $100,000 and be the owner of a fine ranch.

2. Gammel, comp., *Laws of Texas*, VIII, 823, IX, 80–81, 391–395; Gelin, "Organization and Development of Dawson County," p. 29; *Texas Livestock Journal*, Feb. 17, 1883; Slaughter to Harrison, Mar. 17, 1886, interview; *Galveston News*, Feb. 7, 10, 1883; Edmund Thornton Miller, *A Financial History of Texas*,

Bulletin of the University of Texas, No. 37 (Austin, 1916), pp. 333–334, 335; Lester Fields Sheffy, *The Life and Times of Timothy Dwight Hobart, 1855–1935* (Canyon, Tex.: Panhandle-Plains Historical Society, 1950), pp. 74, 79; J. Evetts Haley, "The Grass Lease Fight and Attempted Impeachment of the First Panhandle Judge," *Southwestern Historical Quarterly*, 38 (July 1934), 2.

3. Slaughter to Harrison, Mar. 17, 1886, interview; Small, *Daugherty Land and Cattle Company*; Price, *Open Range Ranching*, map; Gammel, comp., *Laws of Texas*, IX, 883–884, 885–886, 1080.

4. *Texas Livestock Journal*, Mar. 20, 1886, May 12, 1888; Carolyn Bledsoe Goebel, "The Role of Water in the Ranching Industry in the Southwest" (M.A. thesis, Texas Technological College, 1969), pp. 134–165; Fred Horsborough to J. T. Hodges, Sept. 1887, Press Book, II [1887–1888], Spur Ranch Records, Southwest Collection, Texas Tech University; *Texas Almanac, 1976–1977*, p. 164.

5. Lan Franks [Don H. Biggers], *History That Will Never Be Repeated*, reprinted in Seymour V. Connor, ed., *A Biggers Chronicle* (Lubbock: Texas Technological College, 1961), pp. 22–23. This description is attributed to a December 1883 storm, but contemporary sources do not substantiate it. "The worst spell of weather ever known in this part of Texas," according to an Abilene reporter, occurred on January 16, 1885. See *Texas Livestock Journal*, Jan. 24, 31, 1885.

6. O'Keefe, *Cowboy Life*, pp. 98, 99, 101; Jones, "C. C. Slaughter," pp. 16, 17. Slaughter never acknowledged such a loss. The *Texas Livestock Journal* for January 1885 reported a severe snow storm in West Texas but did not mention losses as severe as indicated by O'Keefe and Bob Slaughter.

7. Franks, *History That Will Never Be Repeated*, p. 24; J. W. Williams, "A Statistical Study of the Drouth of 1886," *West Texas Historical Association Year Book*, 21 (1945), 96; Fifth Annual Report, Matador Land and Cattle Company, 1887, Matador Records; Ray Allen Billington, *Westward Expansion* (1949; rpt. New York: Macmillan, 1974), pp. 596–597; *Texas Livestock Journal*, Jan. 28, Feb. 18, 1888.

8. Dale, "Ranching," *Cattleman*, p. 31; Minute Book, Hunter and Evans Land and Cattle Company, pp. 205–296; Berthrong, "Cattlemen on the Cheyenne-Arapaho Reservation," pp. 22–31; Second Annual Report, Matador Land and Cattle Company, 1884, Matador Records; Cox, *Cattle Industry*, p. 150; Powell, *Kansas City's Livestock Trade and Traders*, pp. 43–44; *Texas Livestock Journal*, Aug. 1, 15, 1885, June 11, Oct. 22, 1887; Edward Everett Dale, *The Range Cattle Industry* (Norman: University of Oklahoma Press, 1930), p. 110.

9. Sheffy, *Francklyn Land and Cattle Company*, p. 140; *Texas Livestock Journal*, Aug. 8, 1885, Jan. 30, 1886; "Two-Buckle Ranch," p. 3; Holden, *Espuela Land and Cattle Company*, pp. 59–60; Charles Boone McClure, "A History of Randall County and the T-Anchor Ranch" (M.A. thesis, University of Texas, 1930), p. 81.

10. James A. Wilson, "Cattlemen, Packers, and Government: Retreating Individualism on the Texas Range," *Southwestern Historical Quarterly*, 74 (Apr. 1971), 526; Third Annual Report, Matador Land and Cattle Company, 1885,

Matador Records; *Stock Grower* (Las Vegas, N.M.), Oct 23, 1886, Feb. 19, 1887; Charles Edward Russell, *The Greatest Trust in the World* (New York: Ridgway-Thayer, 1905), p. 10; Gene Gressley, *Bankers and Cattlemen* (Lincoln: University of Nebraska Press, 1974), pp. 160, 261; *Fort Worth Gazette*, Mar. 10, 1887.

11. *Fort Worth Gazette*, Mar. 17, 1887; *Texas Livestock Journal*, Apr. 1–30, 1887; *Stock Grower*, Dec. 1, 1888, Jan 19, 1889.

12. U.S. Senate, *Report of the Select Committee on the Transportation and Sale of Meat Products*, S.R. 829, 50th Cong., 1st sess., 1889, pp. 6, 34–35, 91–92; Cox, *Cattle Industry*, pp. 148–149; U.S. Department of Agriculture, Bureau of Animal Husbandry, *Proceeding of an Interstate Convention of Cattlemen, Held at Fort Worth, Texas, Special Bulletin* (Washington, D.C.: Government Printing Office, 1890), pp. 15, 16.

13. Gressley, *Bankers and Cattlemen*, pp. 263–268; Wilson, "Cattlemen, Packers, and Government," p. 532; Cox, *Cattle Industry*, pp. 136, 139; *Dallas Morning News*, May 5, 1886; *Texas Livestock Journal*, Oct. 1, Nov. 12, 26, 1887.

14. O'Keefe, *Cowboy Life*, p. 104; *Texas Livestock Journal*, Apr. 16, 30, Nov. 26, Dec. 10, 1887.

15. *Texas Livestock Journal*, Mar. 27, 1886, May 1–31, 1887; J. Evetts Haley, *The XIT Ranch of Texas* (Norman: University of Oklahoma Press, 1953), p. 3; Webb & Webb to C. C. Slaughter, Jan. 10, 1886, Louis Hamilton Hill Papers, Southwest Collection, Texas Tech University; *Dallas Morning News*, Mar. 27, May 22, 1886; Marie Sandoz, *The Cattlemen* (New York: Hastings, 1958), pp. 270, 316.

16. *Texas Livestock Journal*, Mar. 27, 1886, Sept. 8, 22, 1888, Mar. 9, 1889; O'Keefe, *Cowboy Life*, pp. 140–142; 163–164; Alley, "Fifty-four Years of Pioneering."

17. O'Keefe, *Cowboy Life*, pp. 181–182; *Encyclopedia of Texas* (Dallas: Texas Development Bureau, 1922), pp. 240, 243, 290–291; Scrapbook, CAS; Walter E. Long, "B Hall of Texas," *Southwestern Historical Quarterly*, 62 (Apr. 1959), 418; Cox, *Cattle Industry*, p. 498; Jones, "C. C. Slaughter," p. 12. Slaughter's sons attended public school in Dallas. George attended Bingham's Military School in North Carolina; E. Dick graduated from the University of Texas in 1893; C. C., Jr., and Alexander from Baylor in 1902 and 1906 respectively. While in college, both E. Dick and C. C., Jr., were coaches of their school clubs' football teams.

5. Royalty on the Range: Ancient Briton and Sir Bredwell

1. Roy Sylvan Dunn, "Drouth in West Texas, 1890–1894," *West Texas Historical Association Year Book*, 37 (1961), 122, 131; *Texas Livestock Journal*, Apr. 4, 1891, June 17, 1892; Looney, "A History of Colorado, Texas," p. 41; Rickard, "Ranch Industry of the South Plains" p. 167.

2. *Texas Livestock Journal*, Apr. 4, 1893, May 11, Oct. 19, 1894; C. C. Slaughter to George M. Slaughter, June 11, Sept. 8, 1894, Jan. 27, 1895, Feb. 21, 1896, George M. Slaughter Papers, Southwest Collection, Texas Tech University (hereafter cited as GMS). The George M. Slaughter Papers, 1893–1959,

contain the largest extant collection of letters written by C. C. Slaughter. Numbering approximately one thousand pieces, the correspondence, primarily between C. C. and George, dates from 1893 to 1910.

3. Scrapbook (microfilm), GMS, original in possession of Mrs. George M. Slaughter II, Roswell, New Mexico; C. C. Slaughter to George M. Slaughter, Jan. 16, 17, 1894, Jan. 2, 27, Feb. 14, 1895, Feb. 21, Mar. 19, 23, Apr. 21, May 5, 1896, GMS; Cox, *Cattle Industry*, p. 126.

4. Donald Abbe, "A History of Lynn County" (M.A. thesis, Texas Tech University, 1974), p. 21; Gelin, "Organization and Development of Dawson County," p. 57.

5. Donald R. Ornduff, *The Hereford in America* (Kansas City: by the author, 1957), pp. 71, 134–135; "A Texas Pioneer," *Cattleman*, 2 (May 1916), 16; Jones, "C. C. Slaughter"; *Texas Livestock Journal*, Sept. 14, Oct. 5, 1894, Oct. 19, 1904; C. C. Slaughter to George M. Slaughter, Sept. 17, 1894, Sept. 17, 1897, GMS; Alvin H. Sanders, *The Story of the Herefords* (Chicago: Breeder's Gazette, 1914), pp. 524–525, 628.

6. Haley, *Charles Goodnight*, p. 318; Goodnight to C. C. Slaughter, Feb. 10, 1894, interview (typescript); C. C. Slaughter to George M. Slaughter, Jan. 15, Apr. 3, 1897, GMS.

7. Sanders, *Story of Herefords*, pp. 609–610, 628, 676; *Texas Stockman and Farmer* (San Antonio), July 14, 1897; C. C. Slaughter to George M. Slaughter, Apr. 2, 1897, Jan. 21, 1898, GMS; Ornduff, *Hereford in America*, p. 136; Hiley T. Boyd, Jr., to David Murrah, June 1, 1970, interview, Oral History File, Southwest Collection, Texas Tech University.

8. Richard Walsh to C. C. Slaughter, Apr. 10, 1897, Walsh to Mrs. John Adair, Apr. 10, 1897, JA Letter Press Book, 1893–1900, Panhandle-Plains Historical Museum, Canyon, Texas; C. C. Slaughter to George M. Slaughter, Feb. 21, 1899, GMS.

9. *Kansas City Drover's Telegram*, as cited in *Texas Stockman and Farmer*, Mar. 15, 1899; Sanders, *Story of Herefords*, p. 675; unidentified newspaper clipping, George M. Slaughter II Papers, in possession of Mrs. George M. Slaughter II; *Morton Tribune*, Aug. 13, 1970; *Western Advocate* (Amarillo), June 29, 1899.

10. C. C. Slaughter to R. C. Burns, Dec. 4, 1897, Feb. 2, 1898, R. C. Burns Papers, Southwest Collection, Texas Tech University; C. C. Slaughter to George M. Slaughter, Oct. 15, 1899, Apr. 17, Dec. 13, 1900, Aug. 1, 1902, Jan. 16, 1906, GMS; Clyde Fitzgerald to Jerry L. Rogers, Apr. 11, 1971, Office Files, Ranching Heritage Center, Texas Tech University; *Roswell Record*, July 15, 1904.

11. C. C. Slaughter to George M. Slaughter, Apr. 13, 15, May 24, 29, 1897, Dec. 28, 1900, GMS; *Livestock World*, June 19, 1902; C. C. Slaughter to George M. Slaughter, Sept. 16, 1902, CCS.

6. The "Indivisible" Empire: The Lazy S Ranch

1. Rickard, "Ranch Industry on the South Plains," p. 109; Gammel, comp., *Laws of Texas*, IX, 351–352, 883–884, X, 63–75; C. C. Slaughter to George

M. Slaughter, Dec. 16, 1893, Sept. 24, 1897, Jan. 21, 1898, GMS; Jean Alexander Paul, "The Farmers' Frontier on the South Plains" (M.A. thesis, Texas Technological College, 1959), pp. 84–85; Alley, "Fifty-four Years of Pioneering"; Deed Records, vol. 1, p. 4, Cochran County Courthouse, Morton, Texas.

2. Cox, *Cattle Industry*, p. 409; C. C. Slaughter to George M. Slaughter, Jan. 21, 25, 1898, GMS; C. C. Slaughter, updated court interrogatory, Hiley T. Boyd Papers, Southwest Collection, Texas Tech University.

3. Deed Trust Records, vol. 1, p. 88, Hockley County Courthouse, Levelland, Texas; Deed Records, vol. 2, pp. 192, 232, 272, 277, 294–295, 313, Cochran County Courthouse; C. C. Slaughter to George M. Slaughter, n.d., June 11, 1900, Feb. 2, July 6, 1901, GMS.

4. C. C. Slaughter to George M. Slaughter, Sept. 22, 1900, Feb. 16, 1901, Jan. 28, May 27, 1904, Oct. 10, 1905, George M. Slaughter to Bob Slaughter, Jan. 10, 1904, George M. Slaughter to G. G. Wright, Jan. 28, 1904, GMS; Deed Records, vol. 3, p. 218, vol. 4, p. 236, vol. 9, p. 278, Hockley County Courthouse.

5. E. Dick Slaughter to George M. Slaughter, Nov. 17, 1900, Feb. 7, 1901, Vest Pocket Book, C. C. Slaughter to George M. Slaughter, Jan. 3, 1901, Sept. 3, 1902, GMS; Deed Records, vol. 2, p. 289, Cochran County Courthouse; George M. Slaughter II to David Murrah, Aug. 25, 1970, interview. For a detailed description of the creation and operation of the Lazy S Ranch, see David J. Murrah, "Cattle Kingdom on Texas' Last Frontier: C. C. Slaughter's Lazy S Ranch" (M.A. thesis, Texas Tech University, 1970), pp. 1–102.

6. Hiley T. Boyd, Jr., to David Murrah, June 4, 20, 1970, interview, Oral History File, Southwest Collection, Texas Tech University; C. C. Slaughter to George M. Slaughter, May 8, 1899, Jan. 23, 1901, GMS; *Texas Stock and Farm Journal* (formerly *Texas Livestock Journal*), Aug. 16, 1899; Inventory, C. C. Slaughter Cattle Company, 1911, Alexander A. Slaughter Papers, Southwest Collection, Texas Tech University (hereafter cited as AAS).

7. *Texas Stock and Farm Journal*, Aug. 16, 1899.

8. "Cattle Raising in Texas: The Great Slaughter Ranches," *Farm and Ranch*, 20 (Feb. 9, 1901), 1–3.

9. C. C. Slaughter to George M. Slaughter, Feb. 14, 1895, June 29, 1897, GMS. As a student at the University of Texas, Dick Slaughter became known as a "hell raiser." While a resident in B Hall, he once pretended to hang himself as part of a practical joke played on the dormitory supervisor. Much to the delight of his college mates, Slaughter "put on an excellent performance of gasping out his last breath while his gallant rescuer frantically administered first aid." Long, "B Hall of Texas," pp. 417–418; see also "Captain E. Dick Slaughter," *Encyclopedia of Texas*, p. 243.

10. Charter and Minutes, C. C. Slaughter Cattle Company (photocopy), Cochran County Historical Museum, Morton, Texas; Legal Materials File, Inventory, C. C. Slaughter Cattle Company, 1911, AAS; E. Dick Slaughter to George M. Slaughter, Feb. 11, 1902, Wright to George M. Slaughter, May 21, 1902, GMS.

11. C. C. Slaughter to George M. Slaughter, Apr. 30, 1898, Sept. 3, Oct. 9,

1902, June 18, 22, 24, July 1, Sept. 27, 1904, George M. Slaughter to C. C. Slaughter, July 1, 1904, GMS; *Encyclopedia of Texas*, p. 243.

12. C. C. Slaughter to George M. Slaughter, June 24, July 1, 1904, Feb. 26, 1910, George M. Slaughter to C. C. Slaughter, Jr., Dec. 17, 1904, Wright to George M. Slaughter, June 3, Aug. 2, 1906, George M. Slaughter to Bob Slaughter, July 29, 1906, GMS; Lee Cooper to David Murrah, June 2, 1970, interview; J. Frank Dobie, "Top Name among America's Cowmen," *San Antonio Light*, Dec. 16, 1956; see also G. G. Wright Correspondence, CCS.

13. C. C. Slaughter to George M. Slaughter, May 21, Aug. 27, 1897, Sept. 22, 1900, June 23, Dec. 10, 1902, unidentified and updated newspaper clipping, "Copy of Offer to O. H. Nelson," May 21, 1897, GMS; Cox, *Cattle Industry*, p. 333; O'Keefe, *Cowboy Life*, p. 208.

14. *Texas Livestock Journal*, Mar. 17, 1893; *Proceedings of the Cattle Raisers Association of Texas, 1896* (Fort Worth: n.p., 1896), pp. 35–36, Averill Scrapbooks, CAS; "The Passing of the Range" (typescript), CCS.

7. The Agrarian Challenge

1. E. Dick Slaughter to George M. Slaughter, Feb. 15, 1901, GMS.

2. Gammel, comp., *Laws of Texas*, X, 1240; Paul, "Farmers' Frontier on the South Plains," p. 86; Patricia Hill Jacobs, "The Texas Lapse Lease Case" (typescript), in possession of Frank Hill, Tahoka, Texas; *Ketner* v. *Rogan*, 68 *Southwestern Reporter* (Tx.), 775 (1902); Texas, *General Laws of the State of Texas Passed at the Regular Session of the Twenty-seventh Legislature* (Austin: Von Boeckman, 1901), p. 195.

3. *Ketner* v. *Rogan*, pp. 774, 776; Wright to George M. Slaughter, June 24, 1902, GMS. Wright was bitter over the loss, attributing it to Colonel Slaughter's leniency. "Keep everybody off the land in your pasture," Wright sternly advised George Slaughter. "Had this method been adopted years ago, his troubles would not now be in existence."

4. C. C. Slaughter to George M. Slaughter, June 18, 21, July 8, Aug. 1, 1902, Oct. 25, 1904, Wright to George M. Slaughter, June 24, 1902, GMS.

5. *General Laws . . . of the Twenty-seventh Legislature*, p. 195; R. D. Holt, "School Land Rushes in West Texas," *West Texas Historical Association Year Book*, 10 (1934), 42–57; W. S. Willis, *A Story of the Big Western Ranches* (Fort Worth: by the author, 1955), pp. 40, 41–42; J. A. Rickard, "South Plains Land Rushes," *Panhandle-Plains Historical Review*, 2 (1929), 98; C. C. Slaughter to George M. Slaughter, Oct. 9, 1902, GMS.

6. Rickard, "South Plains Land Rushes," p. 100; Holt, "School Land Rushes," p. 49; Jot Smyth to Mrs. Frank Miller, Aug. 13, 1959, interview, Oral History File, Southwest Collection, Texas Tech University; *Lamesa Daily Reporter*, Mar. 19, 1953; C. C. Slaughter to George M. Slaughter, Aug. 25, 1903, GMS.

7. Texas, *General Laws of the State of Texas Passed at the Regular Session of the Twenty-ninth Legislature* (Austin: State Printing, 1905), pp. 160–161; Paul, "Farmers' Frontier on the South Plains," p. 88; C. C. Slaughter to George M. Slaughter, Apr. 23, 1898, Sept. 3, 1902, Feb. 28, 1905, GMS; *Big Springs*

Country of Texas, p. 17; *Texas Stockman Journal*, Oct. 18, 1905; Mrs. J. Lee Jones and Rupert N. Richardson, "Colorado City, the Cattlemen's Capital," *West Texas Historical Association Year Book*, 19 (1943), 36–63.

8. C. C. Slaughter to George M. Slaughter, Sept. 20, Dec. 11, 1905, George M. Slaughter to C. C. Slaughter, Apr. 5, 1905, C. C. Slaughter to J. M. Lemons, Dec. 29, 1900, GMS; Boyce Findlay to A. G. Boyce, Aug. 31, 1905, XIT Ranch Records, Archives, Panhandle-Plains Museum; Gressley, *Bankers and Cattlemen*, p. 132.

9. C. C. Slaughter to George M. Slaughter, Dec. 4, 1900, Mar. 10, 1905, Aug. 11, 1906, George M. Slaughter to Wright, Sept. 7, 1905, GMS; David J. Murrah, "From Corset Stays to Cattle Ranching: Charles K. Warren and the Muleshoe Ranch," *West Texas Historical Association Year Book*, 51 (1975), 7.

10. C. C. Slaughter to George M. Slaughter, May 11, Aug. 11, 1906, Mar. 26, Aug. 2, 1907, George M. Slaughter to C. C. Slaughter, Sept. 3, 1907, GMS; Carl Harper, "Movements toward Railroad Building on the South Plains of Texas" (M.A. thesis, Texas Technological College, 1935), p. 84; Billy N. Pope, "The Freighter and the Railroader in the Economic Pattern of Panhandle History" (M.A. thesis, West Texas State College, 1956), p. 54.

11. *Avalanche* (Lubbock), Sept. 20, Oct. 4, 1907, Feb. 14, Apr. 10, 1908; Harper, "Movements toward Railroad Building," pp. 98, 101.

12. George M. Slaughter to C. C. Slaughter, Sept. 3, 1907, GMS; *Avalanche*, Sept. 14, 1907; Keith L. Bryant, Jr., *History of the Atchison, Topeka, and Santa Fe Railway* (New York: Macmillan, 1974), p. 197; Lowell Green and Ernest Wallace, "The Beginning of Slaton, 1911–1913," *West Texas Historical Association Year Book*, 32 (1956), 4.

13. C. C. Slaughter to George M. Slaughter, Dec. 5, 1905, Oct. 19, 1906, Feb. 20, Mar. 3, 1908, GMS; David B. Gracy II, "Selling the Future: A Biography of William Pulver Soash," *Panhandle-Plains Historical Review*, 50 (1977), 7–9; W. P. Soash to Laura V. Hamner, Nov. 15, 1936, interview, Mrs. David C. Gracy Papers, Southwest Collection, Texas Tech University; Marylou McDaniel, *God, Grass, and Grit* (Hereford, Tex.: Pioneer, 1971), pp. 7–9.

14. Gracy, "Selling the Future," pp. 10, 16; Joe R. Baulch, "W. P. Soash on the Urban Frontier of West Texas," *West Texas Historical Association Year Book*, 48 (1972), 24; C. C. Slaughter to George M. Slaughter, Jan. 28, 1909, GMS.

15. C. C. Slaughter to George M. Slaughter, Jan. 28, 1909, GMS; Baulch, "W. P. Soash on the Urban Frontier," p. 25; Gracy, "Selling the Future," pp. 21, 23–24; *Big Springs Country of Texas*, pp. 21–22.

16. C. C. Slaughter to George M. Slaughter, June 28, 1909, June 11, 21, July 6, 1910, GMS; Soash to R. L. Slaughter, Sept. 2, 1909, Soash Papers; Gracy, "Selling the Future," pp. 27, 41, 44–45; Soash to Hamner, Nov. 15, 1936, interview; Baulch, "W. P. Soash on the Urban Frontier," p. 36. Soash's failure did not end his association with the Slaughter family. In 1924 he returned to the South Plains to form the Lone Star Land Company in partnership with several of C. C. Slaughter's children, including Bob, Dick, and Minnie Slaughter Veal. From then until 1943, he sold tracts of both Long S and Lazy S ranches and established the communities of Sundown in Hockley County and Vealmoor in

Howard County, two miles east of the abandoned village of Soash. Soash died in Lubbock in 1961 at the age of eighty-three.

17. C. C. Slaughter to George M. Slaughter, Sept. 3, Dec. 10, 1902, June 8, Nov. 6, 1909, GMS; William L. McDonald, *Dallas Rediscovered: A Photographic Chronicle of Urban Expansion, 1870–1925* (Dallas: Dallas Historical Society, 1978), p. 75; Corporation Record, 1920–1963, Slaughter Building, AAS; Land Book, undated, CCS. The Slaughter Building housed offices of Slaughter heirs until its demolition in 1941. In 1963 the building's site was sold for $487,500. A magnificent office building, One Main Place, occupies the location today.

18. C. C. Slaughter to George M. Slaughter, July 1, 1904, June 8, 1909, GMS; C. C. Slaughter Estate Land Values, Financial Documents, CCS; *San Antonio Light*, Dec. 16, 1956; Mrs. C. C. Slaughter to Alexander A. Slaughter, July 1, 1917, AAS.

19. Alley, "Fifty-four Years of Pioneering"; Elvis E. Fleming, "George M. Slaughter Family," in Elvis E. Fleming and Minor S. Huffman, eds., *Roundup on the Pecos* (Roswell, N.M.: Chaves County Historical Society, 1978), pp. 388–389; C. C. Slaughter to George M. Slaughter, June 8, 1909, Feb. 10, 1910, GMS.

20. Unidentified newspaper clipping, Oct. 5, 1910, Scrapbook, CAS.

8. Banks, Baptists, and the Legacy

1. Rogers, *Lusty Texans of Dallas*, p. 108; *Texas Almanac and State Industrial Guide, 1978–1979*, p. 190; C. C. Slaughter to George M. Slaughter, June 22, 1905, GMS; Report on C. C. Slaughter, Dec. 1, 1912, C. C. Slaughter Company, AAS; Robert E. Tripp, *The First 100 Years: A Brief History of First National Bank in Dallas* (Dallas: First National Bank, 1975), p. 11; Harris, *Dallas: Acorn Planters of Yesteryear*, p. 10; Howard, *Big D Is for Dallas*, p. 52; *Morrison and Fourney's General Directory of the City of Dallas for 1880–1881* (Dallas: Herald, 1880), p. 50.

2. C. C. Slaughter to George M. Slaughter, July 6, 1901, GMS; unidentified newspaper clipping, "Dallas in Gala Garb," newspaper clipping, *Beau Monde*, magazine clipping, Confederate Veterans Reunion Scrapbook, CCS; *Dallas Morning News*, Apr. 30, 1902.

3. B. F. Fuller, *History of Texas Baptists* (Louisville: Baptist Book Concern, 1900), pp. 381–382; McDonald, *Dallas Rediscovered*, p. 47; J. M. Carroll, *A History of Texas Baptists* (Dallas: Baptist Standard, 1923), pp. 821–822, 826; *Baptist Standard* (Waco), Nov. 11, 18, 1897 (Dallas), Nov. 15, 1900; Robert A. Baker, *The Blossoming Desert* (Waco: Word Books, 1970), p. 174; C. C. Slaughter to George M. Slaughter, Nov. 15, 1901, GMS.

4. Powhatan W. James, *Fifty Years of Baylor University Hospital* (Dallas: Baylor University Hospital, 1953), pp. 6, 7, 14, 20, 21, 25–26; Powhatan W. James, *George W. Truett* (New York: Macmillan, 1939), p. 82; Lana Henderson, *Baylor University Medical Center: Yesterday, Today, and Tomorrow* (Waco: Baylor University Press, 1978), p. 28; Rogers, *Lusty Texans of Dallas*, p. 105; George M. Slaughter to C. C. Slaughter, May 11, 1905, C. C. Slaughter to George M. Slaughter, Apr.

3, 1902, Nov. 21, 1905, Oct. 4, 1906, GMS; *Dallas Morning News*, Nov. 23, 1913; Report on C. C. Slaughter, Dec. 31, 1912, C. C. Slaughter Company, AAS; J. B. Cranfill, "Baylor Hospital and Allied Activities," in Carroll, *History of Texas Baptists*, p. 977.

5. Unidentified newspaper clipping, Nov. 25 [?], 1912, Scrapbook, CAS; Wright to Baylor University, Mar. 17, 1916, George W. Truett to C. C. Slaughter, Jan. 17 [16], 1916, CCS; *Dallas Times-Herald*, Jan. 17, 1916.

6. Leon McBeth, *The First Baptist Church of Dallas* (Grand Rapids: Zondervan, 1968), pp. 88–89; *Cranfill et al.* v. *Hayden*, 55 *Southwestern Reporter* (Tx.), 807 (1899); Joseph Martin Dawson, *A Century with Texas Baptists* (Nashville: Broadman Press, 1947), pp. 57, 60; Carroll, *History of Texas Baptists*, pp. 744–746; S. A. Hayden, *The Complete Conspiracy Trial Book* (Dallas: Texas Baptist, 1907), p. 109; *Cranfill et al.* v. *Hayden*, 75 *Southwestern Reporter* (Tx.), 573 (1903); *Baptist Standard*, Nov. 11, 1897, May 12, 19, 1898; J. B. Cranfill, *Dr. J. B. Cranfill's Chronicle* (New York: Fleming H. Revell, 1916), p. 449; Presnall H. Wood and Floyd W. Thatcher, *Prophets with Pens* (Dallas: Baptist Standard, 1969), p. 21; *Worley's Directory of the City of Dallas, 1898* (Dallas: John F. Worley, 1898), p. 43; C. C. Slaughter to George M. Slaughter, May 19, 1898, GMS. Colonel Slaughter was elated with the gesture. "When I looked at that great convention of American Baptists," he noted to George, "I tell you it made me feel mighty proud of my religion. There were assembled there thousands of men whose names are household words, congregated together for the service of Almighty God."

7. Cranfill, *Chronicle*, p. 453; Carroll, *History of Texas Baptists*, p. 800; C. C. Slaughter to George M. Slaughter, May 19, 1898, Feb. 7, July 6, 1901, GMS; *The Hayden-Cranfill Conspiracy Trial* (Dallas: Texas Baptist, n.d.), p. 14; Hayden, *Complete Conspiracy Trial Book*, pp. 27–29, 148; *Cranfill et al.* v. *Hayden*, 55 *Southwestern Reporter* (Tx.), 805, 806 (1899); *Baptist Standard*, Mar. 4, 1900; Fuller, *History of Texas Baptists*, pp. 467–489; *Missionary Worker* (Dallas), Apr. 15, 1901; unidentified newspaper clipping, Nov. 27, 1902, Scrapbook, CAS.

8. J. B. Cranfill, "The Hayden Litigation," in Carroll, *History of Texas Baptists*, pp. 802–804; C. C. Slaughter to George M. Slaughter, Nov. 12, 29, 1902, GMS; unidentified newspaper clipping, Nov. 27, 1902, Scrapbook, CAS; *Cranfill et al.* v. *Hayden*, 80, *Southwestern Reporter* (Tx.), 609 (1904); Wood and Thatcher, *Prophets with Pens*, p. 31; Dawson, *Century with Texas Baptists*, p. 64. In 1901, during the course of the litigation, Hayden joined with other East Texas Baptists in creating the Baptist Missionary Association of Texas, which rivals the Baptist General Convention of Texas.

9. *Baptist Standard*, Oct. 5, 1899; Carroll, *History of Texas Baptists*, pp. 772–814; C. C. Slaughter to George M. Slaughter, Jan. 20, 1905, Apr. 30, 1909, George M. Slaughter to C. C. Slaughter, May 11, 1905, GMS.

10. C. C. Slaughter to George M. Slaughter, Dec. 20, 25, 1894, Dec. 11, 1895, Dec. 10, 1897, Feb. 20, 1908, May 23, 1914, GMS; Rogers, *Lusty Texans of Dallas*, p. 105; Report to the Board of Directors of the C. C. Slaughter Cattle Company for the Fiscal Year Ending December 1, 1915 (photocopy), Cochran County Historical Museum, Morton, Texas.

11. C. C. Slaughter to George M. Slaughter, Jan. 25, 1900, GMS; Rogers, *Lusty Texans of Dallas*, p. 105; unidentified newspaper clipping, Oct. 16, 1912, Scrapbook, CAS; *Dallas Morning News*, Oct. 19, 1913.

12. *Dallas Times-Herald*, June 7, 1914; Report on Bankers' Trust Company, July 31, 1914, folios 29, 46–49, Financial Material, C. C. Slaughter Company, T. D. Gresham to Wright, Jan. 27, 1919, R. L. Slaughter to E. Dick Slaughter, Feb. 8, 1919, AAS; McDaniel, *God, Grass, and Grit*, pp. 9–10; Plan of the Division of the Estate of C. C. Slaughter, Deceased, undated, Legal Documents, CCS; unidentified newspaper clipping, Jan. 11, 1921, Scrapbook, CAS.

13. Rogers, *Lusty Texans of Dallas*, p. 105; Report on C. C. Slaughter Company, Dec. 31, 1915, Dec. 31, 1918, Financial Documents, Report of Special Examination, undated, C. C. Slaughter Cattle Company, Annual Report, June 30, 1921, C. C. Slaughter Cattle Company, AAS.

14. *Houston Post*, Jan. 26, 1919; *Baptist Standard*, Jan. 30, 1919; "Pioneer Cattleman Dies," *Cattleman*, 5 (Feb. 1919), 12; *Dallas Times-Herald*, Jan. 26, 1919; Report on C. C. Slaughter Company, Mar. 31, 1919, AAS; *Dallas Evening Journal*, Jan. 26, 1919.

15. *Dallas Times-Herald*, Jan. 13, 1920; Plan of the Division of the Estate of C. C. Slaughter, Deceased, "To the Officers and Stockholders of the C. C. Slaughter Cattle Company," petition, Aug. 4, 1920, CCS; Ruford Francisco Madera, "The Slaughter Field in Hockley County" (M.S. thesis, Texas Technological College, 1939), p. 1; Carl Coke Rister, "Yates, an 'Oil Klondike,'" *West Texas Historical Association Year Book*, 25 (1949), 9–10; Texas Railroad Commission, *Annual Production by Active Fields, Oil and Gas Division, 1975* (Austin: Railroad Commission, n.d.), p. 80.

16. According to James Cox, the term "cattle king" came into widespread use during the early 1880s. "Newspapers on the lookout for sensational items printed accounts of phenomenal wealth and prosperity of the so-called cattle barons . . . anyone who happened to be located at a hotel in an Eastern town was generally described as 'that well-known cattle king, Mr. _____,' no matter whether the gentleman was a cowboy, a country postmaster, or a small storekeeper." Cox, *Cattle Industry*, p. 136.

17. Atherton, *Cattle Kings*, p. 192; Alley, as quoted in Rickard, "Ranch Industry of the South Plains," p. 182; Edward F. Treadwell, *The Cattle King* (New York: Macmillan, 1931), pp. vii–viii; Donald H. Welsh, "Cosmopolitan Cattle King: Pierre Wibaux," in Michael S. Kennedy, ed., *Cowboys and Cattlemen* (New York: Hastings, 1964), p. 70; Roscoe Sheller, *Ben Snipes: Northwest Cattle King* (Portland, Ore.: Binfords and Mort, 1957), p. 197; Tom Lea, *The King Ranch* (2 vols.; Boston: Little, Brown, 1957), I, 418; Chris Emmett, *Shanghai Pierce* (Norman: University of Oklahoma Press, 1953), p. 7; Haley, *Charles Goodnight*, p. 460.

18. David B. Gracy II, "George Washington Littlefield: A Biography in Business" (Ph.D. dissertation, Texas Tech University, 1971), pp. 95, 105, 138, 219; J. Evetts Haley, *George W. Littlefield, Texan* (Norman: University of Oklahoma Press, 1953), p. 281; Atherton, *Cattle Kings*, pp. 220, 227.

Index

119, on Long S, destroyed by vandals, 110

Wisconsin, 76, 112

Wolfe, G. W., 49

Worth Street (Dallas), 133

Wright, Dela Slaughter, 96, 133, 139

Wright, Ed Dela, 139

Wright, Florence Roberta, 139

Wright, G. G., 88, 95–96, 139, 154; defends lapse leasing, 105; ideas of, 106; manages real estate, 120; negotiates suit settlement, 127

Wright, G. G., Jr., 139

Wright, Jowell Slaughter, 139

Wright, Stuart Phillips, 139

Wyoming, 54, 70, 72

XIT Ranch, 47, 65–67, 136; closes shipping facilities, 111; established, 45; lands colonized by W. P. Soash, 115; largest ranch in West Texas, 41

Yellow House Canyon, 66

Yellow House Ranch, 136

Yoakum County, Texas, 104

Young County, Texas, 8, 13, 28, 40, 44; Indian raids in, 11, 22; population increase in, 39

Yuma, Arizona, 129

Zavala County, Texas, 88